THE MAKING OF A MEDIUM

The Making of a Medium

*Clairvoyance, Spirit Communication,
and Physical Mediumship*

Elaine M. Kuzmeskus

2011
Galde Press
Lakeville MN
www.galdepress.com

Third Edition
First Printing, 2011

Galde Press
PO Box 460
Lakeville, Minnesota 55044–0460
www.galdepress.com

This book is dedicated to my husband,
Ronald Kuzmeskus,
and our four children
Adam, Heather, Kimberly and Michael.

Author Elaine M. Kuzmeskus.
Certified as a medium by the National Spiritualist Association of Churches

About the Author
Elaine M. Kuzmeskus

Elaine Kuzmeskus, director of the New England School of Metaphysics, is a nationally known Spiritualist medium. Born with the gift of clairvoyance, she made contact with her Hindu guide at age four:

"Ever since I was in my crib, I had been fascinated by spirits. When I was about four, a Hindu gentleman only I could see started giving me instructions from the other side. 'Cross your fingers and place them over the middle of your forehead. Now concentrate and push the energy out.' Soon I was able to visualize people and see them in their future state Other guides quickly followed: an Egyptian master and an ancient Chinese doctor."

In 1972, Elaine Kuzmeskus was certified by the National Association of Spiritualist Churches as a medium. During her thirty-five years of mediumship, she has conducted many well-publicized séances, including the 1997 Official Houdini Séance at the Goodspeed Opera House in Haddam, Connecticut, and a séance for the cast of the play *Blithe Spirit* at the Long Wharf Theatre in New Haven, Connecticut. In 2004, Professor Kuzmeskus published *Soul Cycles*, a text which combines keen psychological insight with the ancient science of astrology. She also completed the book *Connecticut Ghosts* which is based on mediumship, psychic photography and local legends. Her third book, *Séance 101: Physical Links to the Other Side*, explores the fascinating world of physical mediumship from the raps of Fox sisters to today's psychic photography, electronic voice phenomena and trumpet séances. In 2009, she was featured on the PBS special *Things That Go Bump*.

Contents

Acknowledgments

I would like to acknowledge two main influences: Edgar Cayce and Paramahansa Yogananda. From the study of Edgar Cayce's work I learned "The psychic of the soul." As I read Yogananda's *Autobiography of a Yogi*, I discovered how to connect with the Cosmic Mind through the practice of meditation. After several months of daily meditation, spirit guided me to Rev. Kenneth Custance and Rev. Gladys Custance, two veteran mediums who helped me to unfold the gift of mediumship. Their patience and wisdom were always evident in their Friday night unfoldment circle.

I also with to thank my husband, Ronald Kuzmeskus,for his support of my spiritual journey, even though the path has not always been smooth. (It seldom is!) I also wish to thank the students of the New England School of Metaphysics for their many thoughtful questions regarding the development of mediumship, which I hope I have answered in this volume. Finally, I would like to thank my editor, Susan Roberts, for her kind assistance that has kept the book on course; and Phyllis Galde, president of Galde Press, for her dedication to publishing "quality books that make a difference."

Chapter One

A Modern Initiate

Politics without principles, education without character, science without humanity, and commerce without morality are not only useless, but positively dangerous.

—Sathya Sai Baba

EVER SINCE I was in my crib, I have been a medium. When I was about four, a Hindu gentleman only I could see made his appearance. By five, my Hindu guide was giving me instructions: "Cross your fingers and place them over the middle of your forehead." As I did so, I saw what looked like a tunnel of dark light. "Now concentrate and push the energy forward." he continued. I did and soon I was able to visualize people and see them in their future state.

Before I knew it, the bare-chested Hindu with the white turban was predicting my future as well. Some of the advice seemed to come out of the blue. For example, when I caught a glance of our next-door neighbor's son (a disabled Korean vet) bandaging the stump of his amputated leg, my guide telepathically told me, "Don't turn away. Someday you may marry a man who has lost his leg." I felt a rush of compassion for the boy.

1

Later I learned that my future husband, Ronald Kuzmeskus, who was seven at the time, almost lost his leg when he was fourteen. When he developed severe blood poisoning, the doctors told his parents it would be necessary to amputate the infected leg in order to save him. His father, a practical man, said "I don't want a son without a leg," and refused to grant permission to operate. Apparently, the angels were on his side, as Ron survived intact.

I love this story because it shows that the future is not fixed. Just as the traffic reporter who sits in the helicopter, hovering above the highway, can accurately give details about the morning commute, so guides can see the road ahead. We always have freedom to take an alternate route. However, it is up to us to make the best choice. In Ron's case, his father made the final decision and his angels took over.

Even before I was born the angels seemed to be looking over my shoulder. My father, Ted Marshall, was separated from his troops in the South Pacific during World War II. For several weeks he and his fellow soldiers survived on whatever vegetation they could scrounge. His weight dropped from 165 to 135 pounds on his five-foot-ten-inch frame. While he survived the ordeal—he never ate salad again. Years later, when Lily Dale medium, Rev. Sherry Lee Calkins, solemnly explained: "Your angels had to save your father's life before you were born, so you could come in," I felt a chill go down my back.

While angels come to assist us, they do not take over. All my lessons (and there were many), I had to learn the hard way. One of the saddest events in my childhood was the sudden death of my beloved grandmother. No one understood me like Nana. No wonder, she was quite psychic herself. When she read the cards for family amusement, she could be most accurate. When Uncle John was dating Aunt Polly, Nana cordially read her cards. "Oh, I see a lovely pair of gloves, some stockings and a ring coming!" My uncle (a nonbeliever) was furious with his mother, for giving away all his Christmas gifts! Nana, of course, staunchly objected —"I didn't peek at the presents. I just read the cards."

My grandmother was really my first teacher. Her cheerful acceptance of spirit rubbed off on me. Nana would always say, "You don't have to be afraid of the dead. It is the people who are alive that you have to fear."

I was fortunate my family was open to spirit communication and even reincarnation. Eagerly I would listen to my grandparents as they sat at the kitchen table in our Dorchester, Massachusetts, apartment to discuss each new segment of the *Boston Herald's* series on the reincarnation of Bridey Murphy. No wonder that by the time I was ten I was having dreams of another life in Virginia in the 1800s as a widow abandoned by her four sons. Later that year when Nana died, my interest in the psychic lessened, for there was really no one to share it with.

Life was grim without Nana's cheerful banter, tasty desserts and Sunday outings. Grampa valiantly carried on, but his own health deteriorated. Suddenly, home was no longer a safe haven.

By the time I was eighteen, I was only too happy to begin classes at the University of Massachusetts in Boston. Soon, my Hindu guide was back as well. One day as I was getting out of the shower, I saw a twelve-inch square of cobalt blue beside an identical-sized square in Kelly green. I just "knew" I was being guided.

A more positive and idealistic mood replaced my childhood grief. For one thing, I made up my mind to live my faith fully. That included a belief in nonviolence toward all beings. Soon, I was joining antiwar protesters on the Boston Commons. Like many students in 1967, I felt the Vietnam War was an unjust one waged for oil. One of the last pieces of legislation that John F. Kennedy had signed was a bill to have all of our troops out by 1965. Sadly, President Johnson, who many voted in because he stated "I am not going to send American boys to war Vietnam boys should be fighting" first act was to reverse Kennedy's bill to get the troops out in two years. Why? The only reason seemed to enhance special interests. "How could oil be worth the death of innocent civilians?" I thought, as I glanced at the *Time* magazine cover which featured a picture of a pretty nude Vietnamese girl screaming as she was struck by napalm.

My stance for nonviolence hardened as I protested the war. I even made up my mind not to participate in dissecting a live frog, as required in the biology lab. I would rather flunk biology than torture an animal. When I entered the second floor lab, my professor, a red-headed young woman fresh out of Radcliffe, took one look at my solemn face and grabbed my frog, saying "We will use Miss Marshall's frog for demonstration." Don't ask me how, but I just knew she *knew* I wasn't going to dissect the squirming frog.

About my junior year in college, I began to meditate in earnest. Every day at the same time, I would light a candle in the apartment I shared with two other girls in Brookline, Massachusetts. After staring at the flame, I would close my eyes and concentrate on the after image. At first it was just the image of a red flame, then a blue flame and finally a white. With the white oval, symbols and faces appeared. Soon the flame became a portal to the other side. It wasn't long before I came in contact with a man in a wheelchair who had lost both legs. Telepathically, I heard him say, "I am your relative."

Next to him was a tiny old woman with a purple flower in her hand. "That's my name," she said, and the vision faded. I asked my mother, I " Did we ever have a relative who lost his legs?" "Yes," Momma answered. "My grandfather. Grandpa Brickett had diabetes and lost both of his legs a year before he died. When he lived in Vermont, his housekeeper, Violet, took care of him."

Whether I knew it or not, I was on my way to becoming a professional medium in the summer of 1969. It was a year when America thought anything was possible. As the Beatles sang, "All we need is love", American youth "tuned in, turned on and dropped out." I spent the spring of 1969 finishing my thesis on James Joyce and marching in Viet Nam protest rallies on the Boston Common. By June I had obtained a B.A. in English from the

University of Massachusetts, and I too decided to "drop out" by cheerfully incinerating all my college notes!

The timing was right. During my last two years in college, I had spent more time reading metaphysical books than Shakespeare. My reality was changing faster than the times. Not quite sure what my future might hold, I took a sabbatical of sorts that summer.

In July, a spur-of-the-moment trip to Maine was to alter the course of my life forever. While perusing a local Bangor newspaper, I spotted a small announcement at the back: "Opening services for the First Spiritualist Camp of Etna Maine Sunday at 2:00 p.m." I had to go! I found my way to Camp Etna and had my first reading with the Rev. Bill Ellis. He told me many things: I had a lot of yellow in my aura, an older lady was in back of me (Nana), and I was not going to marry the man I was seeing at the time. All seemed plausible, but I shrugged as the Rev. Ellis said, "I know you don't believe me, but someday you will be doing this work."

Sure enough, a month later I was enrolled in a development circle. I was searching in earnest for the answers to life's questions: Who am I? Why am I here? At the same time that I joined a Spiritualist circle, I signed up for yoga classes at the local YMCA and also entered the New England School of Astrology. When other twenty-two-year-olds were dating, I was meditating doing charts and talking to spirits.

It is not surprising that with all this inner work and no outer income, I soon ran out of money. It seemed the spiritual life had its challenges. My roommate, Pauline, was not amused when I told her I was going to be late on the rent. Quite frankly, I was not sure how I was going to pay the rent that month, as I had no job. For the past previous three months, I had been subsisting on a small inheritance of $300 from my grandfather. Now that money had dwindled to about five dollars and change. I prayed. I meditated. I read *Autobiography of a Yogi* in earnest that night before I went to sleep. I truly felt the loving presence of its author, Paramahansa Yogananda, as I turned out the light. The next morning I was awakened by a phone call from the Boston public schools. "Can you substitute today?"

"Yes, I certainly can," I answered. I loved being a sub. Not only did it pay the bills, but it also allowed ample time off for my spiritual pursuits.

Two books greatly influenced me during those days. One was *Autobiography of a Yogi* and the other was *The Sleeping Prophet* by Jess Stearn. The "sleeping prophet" was Edgar Cayce, a man who had died before I was born, but he seemed to be the only person I knew of who also saw colors and spoke with dead people. He explained that there were many spirits in the lower realms close to the earth. The task of the meditator was to rise above the sea of faces. When I saw a crowd of spirits seeking to get my attention during candle meditation, I ignored the sea of faces and sought a higher sphere. That's when I met my great-grandfather and his housekeeper. My tie with Cayce was a deep one. We were both drawn to ancient Egypt. In the Cayce readings, he had been told that he was the priest Ra-Ta. In a vision, I saw myself as an Egyptian initiate, lying still in a huge sarcophagus. I knew then that it was my destiny to be a medium.

Still, I had never met a psychic until my first reading with Rev. William Ellis in July of 1969 at the First Spiritualist Camp of Etna, Maine. Rev. Ellis, a spry man in his sixties, explained, "There are seven planes and each plane has seven planes so there are forty-nine in all." His guide from the seventh plane had told him my aura was yellow (my favorite color) and announced that my present boyfriend and I were not getting along (true) and accurately described Nana who had died when I was ten.

When I left Camp Etna, I took some Spiritualist literature with me. I immediately noticed that there was a development circle in Brookline, Massachusetts, where I was living at the time. Of course I had to go. The person I met at the circle was Rev. Kenneth Custance, a distinguished silver-haired medium. I immediately trusted him, something I do not usually do. Soon, I was a regular at the Friday circle hosted by his wife, Rev. Gladys Custance, a trance medium.

They were a unique duet, for both were accomplished harpists,

Spiritualist mediums, and ordained ministers. Always impeccably dressed, the two made a regal couple. Gladys had a Hindu guide named the Professor. It was really the Professor who conducted the classes. His instruction on affirmations and meditation proved invaluable. Soon I was experiencing the most extraordinary meditation sessions.

Mediumship training took about three years. However, it was not all smooth sailing. After two years with the Custances, I was almost killed in a car accident. Prior to the accident, I had a disturbing dream—Gladys, came through in the dream state. As she watched me pick at a splinter in the sole of my foot, she advised, "Don't pick at it. Let it go." Too late, I was already digging the splinter out with a needle. To my surprise, a cobra came out of the tiny scratch and bit me in the third eye!" Two weeks later, I was almost killed in a car crash which broke my clavicle in three places, one piece about an inch above my heart.

The experience left me in limbo as I was training at the time to become a Spiritualist healer. How could I possibly do any healing with a pin in my clavicle and a cast on my left shoulder? I couldn't even drive. Fortunately, fellow astrologer Mary Letorney and her husband were kind enough to take me in. Blessed by their support, I was able to spend many an hour meditating while waiting for the shoulder to heal.

Of course I was despondent. My appetite was nil. There seemed little to do except to fast and pray for guidance. One day, I awoke to see "Paracelsus" written in green letters floating in front of my eyes. When I looked the name up, it was that of a doctor who lived in Europe in the late 1500s. Since Paracelsus believed nature had the power to heal and often suggested that food had curative powers, I broke my fast with a bowl of spaghetti! Little by little, my appetite improved and my depression lifted.

Next, I wrote a letter to Gladys, asking, "Since I am unable to do any more healing for awhile, would it be possible to study for mediumship certification instead?" I nervously mailed the letter to her winter residence, Camp Cassadaga in Florida. Mrs. Custance could be unyielding in spiritual matters, so I had no idea what she would reply. In about a month, I got an affirmative reply much to my relief. Six months later, April 23, 1972, I passed my test service, the final step in becoming a medium.

The date, in fact, had been predicted during an astral travel experience about three years before, with my Hindu master. He instructed me in astral travel, and after the initial few breaths, I felt my spirit leave through my third eye and float through the ceiling. As I picked up in acceleration, I felt dizzy. Within minutes, I was drifting over India and then landed in a beautiful pool of turquoise water. When I glanced around, there was my Hindu guide. Telepathically, he indicated that I look at a newspaper about twenty feet away. "Draw it near with your third eye," he advised. Concentrating on my third eye, the Sunday edition of the *Boston Globe* was beneath my eyes, with the date April 23 clearly visible. It seems the Hindu had definite plans for me. Three years later, on April 23, 1972 I passed the mediumship service, the final requirement for a certified medium.

Once I received my papers, I was determined to work as a medium. Even after I later married and had four children, I continued to serve the First Spiritualist Church of Onset, as well as local churches in Connecticut and Springfield, Massachusetts. Eventually, I divided my time between my medium office and the college classroom where I taught psychology.

Psychology and mediumship can complement each other, especially grief counseling, which many clients seek. After I had been a medium for a couple of years, I began to realize that some clients needed more than affirmations. Some were seriously troubled and needed psychological guidance. For me it was not enough to bring through the spirit of a dead father. I also wanted to help people through their grief and depression.

In psychology, I was to learn that death, according to Freud, is the prototype for all anxiety. Our fear of death is the deepest fear we face. How sad, I thought. It is really just a transition to another world. I don't think my professors would have approved of mediumship. In fact, I knew they didn't. When we were asked to write out greatest fear on a card and place it in the box, I wrote, "I am the most afraid that people will find out that I am a medium." The professor, who by the way was my adviser, knew I was the one who wrote the card. He accused me of taking counseling training as a foil for mediumship. Nothing could be further from the truth. I believe both are valid. It is comforting to know that we exist past the change called death, however some still need psychological help in times of grief and confusion.

Not only did I remain in the program, but I graduated in May of 1978 with a master's in counseling from the University of Hartford in Connecticut. Since then I have obtained a license as an LPC, a Licensed Professional Counselor. While I realize that mediumship and medicine are worlds apart, this was not always the case. Hippocrates, the father of medicine, for example, was known to consult oracles. The ancient Greeks really revered their oracles.

Even though I trained as a counselor, I still focused on mediumship, teaching evening classes in psychology and parapsychology. By 1997, I was approached by the Goodspeed Opera House to be the medium for the upcoming Houdini Séance. While I was flattered, I usually do not conduct public séances. Just as I was about to decline the invitation, I felt a strong male presence in back of me. Unsure of what answer to give, I told the manager I would think about it for a week. I had mixed feelings about doing the Houdini Séance. My first concern was that the very public séance would be too sensational and my second was that Houdini may have reincarnated or simply may not have wished to return.

After a week of reflection, I decided to decline the offer. However, the spirit that had appeared over my left shoulder had other plans. As I brushed my hair, I felt the same presence that had been there during my conversation with the Goodspeed Opera House. This time his gentle voice came in clearly: "Houdini has a message for you." Suddenly, I realized it was the medium who had brought the spirit Harry Houdini through to his wife, Bess none other than Arthur Ford. Of course, I accepted. For the record, I believe that Harry Houdini did make a brief appearance at the 1997 Official

Houdini Séance. He came in spirit with a well-timed message for Timothy Gulan, the actor who portrayed him in the play *Houdini*.

About the time I conducted the Houdini seance, I began to take classes in astral travel and trance mediumship at Lily Dale Assembly in upstate New York. In 1999, I took a seminar in astral travel with Carol Gasper at Lily Dale which was remarkable. I will never forget the incredible light I felt around me and the sight of loving presences of a spiritual master. During the astral travel, I found myself immersed in light on a higher plane with Saint Francis. The slender image in a roughly fashioned brown -hooded habit tied at the waist with a piece of rope sent a chill throughout my whole body. The loving-kindness that radiated from Saint Francis has always been an inspiration, but there was nothing to compare with actually seeing him face to face.

Since then, I have presented my own seminars at Lily Dale Assembly. Each summer I make the seven-hour trek to upstate New York to serve as a guest medium. People flock to Lily Dale from all over the country and Canada. It is a pleasure to give seminars on dreams and astral travel, astrology, and physical mediumship to sincere seekers.

I have also written three books: *Soul Cycles*, *Connecticut Ghosts*, and *Séance 101*. My favorite is *Séance 101*, as it deals with physical mediumship. Naturally, I felt many guides come to assist me as I researched the topic. In recent years, my research has taken me to Camp Chesterfield in Indiana; the Arthur Findlay College in Stansted, England; and John of God's compound in Brazil. Over the years, I have progressed from a mental medium to a trance medium and added some physical mediumship, such table tipping and psychic photography.For the most part, the journey has been a pleasant one.

However, mediumship can be hard work, especially if you are dealing with a parent who has lost a child or someone who is terminally ill. While it is not an easy assignment, I still view mediumship as a sacred task, one guided by spirit. In these days of psychic hotlines and greedy gypsies, it would be easy to become disheartened and forget the many compassionate mediums who serve daily.

For those who are tempted to take shortcuts, I would remind them of this quote from the Indian guru Sai Baba: "Politics without principles, education without character, science without humanity, and commerce without morality are not only useless, but positively dangerous." I would add that mediumship without ethics can also be dangerous.

Wedding picture of my parents, Theodore and Dorothy Marshall.
Left to right: Aunt Evelyn Marshall, Mother, Father, Uncle John Brickett.

Author around the age she began to communicate
with her Hindu guide. Two-year-old sister Barbara on the left.

Author Elaine Marshall, May 1972, when she was certified as
a medium by the National Spiritualist Association of Churches.

Chapter Two

Death, God's Other Door

For what is it to die but to stand naked in the wind and to melt into the sun? And what is it to cease breathing, but to free the breath from its restless tides, that it may rise and expand and seek God unencumbered? —Kahlil Gibran

YOUR LOVED ONES are only a thought away, as they continue to exist in a world beyond this one. Spiritualists such as Andrew Jackson Davis like to think of the other side as a peaceful place, a Summer Land not unlike the ancients Greeks who referred to the land beyond death as Elysian Fields. American Indians described the afterlife as the happy hunting ground.

Whatever name it is given, the other side has been a topic of fascination ever since the pharaohs built the pyramids. The largest pyramid—the Great Pyramid of Giza—covers 13 acres, originally stood over 481 feet high, made of stone blocks that average over two tons apiece. Its interior is as amazing as its dimensions. Egyptian kings filled the inner-most chambers with treasures then sealed them with incantations and secured them in secret passages in preparation for the afterlife. These monuments were not just tombs. They were places of initiation into a new life beyond the earth plane. For instance, the empty sarcophagus in the King's Chamber of the Great Pyramid symbolized the commonly held view of the Egyptians that there is no death.

Both the ancient Egyptians and Tibetans wrote books giving detailed instruction on the journey to the other side. Tibetans showed an intimate knowledge of death in *The Tibetan Book of the Dead*. As in *The Egyptian Book of the Dead*, death is not viewed as an end but as transition. According to *The Tibetan Book of the Dead*, the spirit must pass through six bardos, which range from the first bardo, the moment of birth, to the sixth bardo, the moment of rebirth. In between, people experience the second bardo from birth to adulthood, followed by the third bardo from adulthood to the moment of death.

At death, the soul enters the fourth bardo, where it merges with the white light of Dharmala. Stephen Levine, author of *Who Dies?* likens the fifth bardo to a place of peaceful and wrathful deities: "It is here one meets the ten thousand loving and ten thousand wrathful aspects of mind." Once there, the soul must decide whether or not to return to earth in order to learn more lesson of life. If the soul does decide to return, then the person reincarnates in the sixth bardo.

Even today, Tibetans take death very seriously. Tibetan Buddhists believe those who are with us on our deathbed will be with us in the next life as well. When a person is close to death, a Tibetan priest visits the home of the dying person to assist in the journey into the next bardo. The priest remains until the person passes over and then prays for the soul of the departed for forty days to help the newly departed through the bardos, lest he or she return too soon. While old souls, such as the Dalai Lama, may come back quickly to aid humanity, other souls need more time before choosing their next incarnation. Tibetans maintain a lineage of spiritual leaders such as the Dalai Lama and other high priests by persistently searching for them as they return in successive incarnations.

From Egypt and Tibet, civilization progressed westward into Greece and Rome. Both cultures believed in the afterlife and the presence of gods as protectors. The Greeks viewed heaven as Elysian Fields, a land of perpetual spring and happiness. They worshiped many gods and evoked the spirits of the dead in healing rituals. Greek philosopher Plato believed everything had a soul, including plants, animals and even planets. Socrates, his teacher, was so secure in his belief in the afterlife that he preferred to drink a deadly cup of hemlock rather than face the wickedness of a corrupt court. His last words; "We owe a cock to Asclepius: pay it without fail." Thus he indicated a desire to pay homage to death by giving the Greek god of healing a gift.

Jesus also believed very much in life beyond earthy existence: "In my father's house there are many mansions." The early Christians, particularly the Gnostics, had a strong belief in life after death and reincarnation. In Matthew, Jesus was asked upon healing the blind man, "Lord, was it his fault or his parents?" The very question indicates that the belief in reincarnation was commonplace. If the parents had neglected the blind man as child, it would be their fault. However, if the fault was with the blind man himself, then his blindness would have been the result of a past life. Unfortunately, the Council of Nicaea in A.D. 325 removed many portions of the Bible that made reference to reincarnation. Later, the Emperor Justinian in A.D. 543 removed all references to reincarnation and any mention of preexistence from the Bible. During the Dark Ages, which followed the Gnostic writings were lost and any mention of reincarnation was considered heresy by the church, now dominated by Catholic bishops and the Pope.

It wasn't until the 1850s that Christianity received a major challenge in the form of Spiritualism and Theosophy. Both groups offered plausible explanations for "the change called death." Spiritualism began in 1848 in

Hydesville, New York, when two young sisters, Kate and Maggie Fox, began communicating with the spirit of a deceased peddler. The spirit rappings constituted evidence to many that there is no death and there are no dead, a tenet of the National Spiritualist Association of Churches. The organization, however, does not endorse reincarnation, primarily because it was not a tenet of Rev. Andrew Jackson Davis.

Theosophists, on the other hand, do believe in reincarnation. Founded by Madame Helena Blavatsky, the Theosophical Society believes in the brotherhood of man and the study of the powers latent in man. Channeling the words of the masters, Madame Blavatsky wrote in *The Secret Doctrine*: "Man must know who he was before he arrives at who he is." Theosophy emphasizes the power of thought. Mental change even at death is possible:

> Mental change or glimpses of spiritual truth may make a man suddenly change to the truth even at death thus creating good skandas (seeds) for the next life… But the karmic effects of the past life must follow; for man in the next birth must pick up the skandas or vibratory impressions that he has left in Astral light.—H.P. Blavatsky, *The Secret Doctrine*, p. 589

Later theosophists Geoffrey Hodson and C. W. Leadbeater have added to the literature. Hodson, gave this advice on preparing for death:

> Can one make plans for one's life after the death of the body? Certainly one can, for as I have just said, the law of cause and effect operates from physical to super-physical life. Each one of us, therefore, is continuously making his after-death conditions by his daily thoughts, motives, feelings, words, and deeds. If we live nobly and beautifully and unselfishly while on earth, we ensure for ourselves a corre-

sponding measure of happiness in the hereafter.—Geoffrey
Hodson, *Through the Gateway of Death,* p. 36

According to Leadbeater, author of *The Masters and the Path* and *The Inner Life*, the time of death is not always fixed. If there is a spiritual benefit, part of a larger karma, the Lords of Karma may allow more time on earth. Leadbeater likens karma to a cup. When one begins a new life, one spoonful is taken from the cup. However, a soul may choose to work out more karma and hence remain longer in the body. This is why some souls are saved miraculously, if it is not their time to go.

Shortly after the birth of Spiritualism and Theosophy in the early 1900s, Edgar Cayce, the sleeping prophet, began his work. Cayce, clairvoyant as a child, always saw auras around people. Once when he was about to enter the elevator of a skyscraper, he saw no auras over the heads of the occupants. The startled Cayce stepped back, letting the elevator door close without his entering. Within minutes, the elevator cable snapped, and all aboard plunged to their deaths!

Fortunately, Edgar Cayce survived to continue his trance channeling, which included many readings on death and dying. Cayce's guide, known simply as the Source, continually advised that the present life is only a stage in our evolution. "Death as commonly spoken of is only the passing through God's other door."

What really happens at the time of death? The astral body separates from the physical body. This is a natural occurrence, one which takes place every night in sleep. However in death the detachment is permanent as the silver cord of life, which is attached to our spirit body, is severed. The spirit body floats above the physical and observes. For example, Jean Loomis, a Connecticut psychic, went into cardiac arrest during routine surgery and described her near death experience. She found herself hovering above her body and saw her doctor frantically doing CPR on her lifeless body. She felt no physical pain. Then her doctor threw a sheet over her saying, "It's useless, she's dead" to the young intern with a pony tail next to him. The determined intern, pulled the sheet back and started doing CPR. Immediately, Jean was back in her body "all because of an intern with a pony tail."

Those who go further into the near-death experience hear a ringing or buzzing and feel the sensation of going through a long tunnel with a light at the end, according to experts like Dr. Raymond Moody and Dr. Kenneth Ring. In *The Omega Project*, Ring outlines the stages of a near-death experience. First, there is a separation from the body. If the person has been in pain, the suffering is gone. Next, the dying person goes through a tunnel toward a bright light, often feeling a sense of peace. Loved ones and guides are there to greet the individual. Often the person is told to return, and that it is not yet their time to pass over at which point the soul returns to the body.

One of the most amazing cases of near-death experiences was that of Dannion Brinkley, who was struck by lightening on September 17, 1975. During his out-of-body state, Brinkley met "beings of light" who showed him 117 future events, 95 of which have already come true. In one vision, he saw a president dressed as a cowboy, with the initials R.R. being elected in 1980 (Ronald Reagan), and he saw a nuclear power plant blowing up with the name Wormwood. ("Chernobyl" means "wormwood" in Ukrainian.) Other predictions have yet to come true.

He predicted in 1992 a secret alliance was to be made between China. Saudi Arabia, and Syria to destroy the West's economy, particularly that of the United States. He saw in 1995 poison around a land mass reminiscent of Norway. A war between Russia and China and natural and unnatural catastrophes have also been predicted by Brinkley. There is a disclaimer, however; the beings of light told him these events were not inscribed in stone. They could be avoided if humans changed their ways.[1]

Another aspect of the near-death experience is the life review. When I was teaching a class in death and dying, one of the students, a fireman, told the class of his own life review. The fireman went back into a burning build-

Edgar Cayce, America's Sleeping Prophet.

ing to bring his buddy out. Once inside, he found his fellow fireman uncon-scious. As the fire fighter lifted his fallen comrade, the retaining wall in back of him collapsed, leaving no escape route. "My life flashed in front of my eyes. I was sure I was going to die," he told his classmates. "I knew my num-ber was up and I started praying. Just then I looked up and saw a helicop-ter overhead." Fortunately, both men were rescued when the pilot threw down a line.

Another amazing rescue occurred in India when Sai Baba, whom many consider an Indian avatar, interceded on behalf of an American, Walter Cowan. Cowan's, wife, Elsie requested a healing for her ailing husband. Sadly, Walter passed over before Swami could return to the ashram. His faithful wife kept vigil by the body, until others in the ashram insisted the body be taken to the morgue. When Sai Baba returned, he went to the local mortu-ary and went in alone to view the body. An hour later, Walter Cowan, very alive walked out of the room and asked Elsie for a cup of tea! Of course, when he returned to the ashram, everyone wanted to know what it was like on the other side. Walter Cowan described being in a huge hall with many other people waiting to see a judge seated in the front of the hall. Sai Baba came in and pleaded with the judge for Cowan's life. Finally the judge agreed to let Walter return. Within minutes he was back in in his body. Returning to the earth, Walter Cowan said, "was like returning to a sewer!" He lived another year happily with Elsie, before he returned to the Hall of Judgment.

People who return from the other side like Walter Cowan report no fear of death. I know this firsthand as I had my first brush when I was ten years old. At the time, my sister Barbara and my mother and I were living with my maternal grandparents Harry and Kathryn Brickett in Dorchester, Massachusetts. We all thought the separation would be temporary until my mother received a note from my father, Ted Marshall, in LA asking for a divorce. Despondent, Momma began to spend increasing time away from home with her friends.

Happily for us, our grandparents stepped in to raise us. One evening I went to bed with severe stomach pains. My mother as usual was out with friends and left no contact information, to my grandparents dismay. As their concern for me mounted, I overheard Nana say to Grandpa, "What if it is an appendicitis attack? What can we do? If we take Elaine to the hospital, they might not operate without her mother's signature. She could die."

Being a child, I took my grandmother's word literally. My last thought before I drifted off to sleep was "I could die." Soon I was on the other side and my Hindu guide was there to assist me. Within seconds I was drawn a hundred years back in time. I saw an old lady about seventy with gray hair neatly pulled back in a bun and dressed in a long cotton skirt with a prairie bonnet on her head. There was something familiar about the face, In a strange way the features of her face resembled mine. Then I realized that the woman was someone I had been in a past life.

Next, I entered this long-ago consciousness. It was early morning and this elderly lady with a wooden bucket in hand was on her way down the hill to draw water from the well. She seemed resigned to the fact her husband had died and her four sons had all left. There was a feeling a loneliness. Then, without warning, the old woman suffered a massive heart attack. She dropped her bucket as her physical body fell back and her spirit body went forward. "There is nothing to death, I thought. You just drop your body."

Then the calm face of my Hindu guide appeared. "Remember what you have seen," he said solemnly. By the way, I must have had a healing of some sort, as the next morning, I was fine.

My second brush with death came just as I was in the process of becoming a medium. In November of 1972, I was en route to a job interview for an English teaching position at Avon High School when my car was struck broadside. For weeks before the accident, I felt something was amiss. Two weeks later, I was almost killed in a car crash which broke my clavicle into three places, on piece about an inch above my heart Fortunately after several months of recuperation under the care of kind friends, I was able to resume Mrs. Custance's Friday night circle.

Now that I a practicing medium, I encounter all types of deaths. When an elderly or very ill person passes, death comes as a relief. However, those who die suddenly often regret not being able to say good-bye to those they love.

This is especially true for victims of homicide. Often they report feelings of anger toward those who took their life. The saddest death, though, is a suicide. Frequently these souls take their lives because they view death as an end to their suffering or because they feel the world would be better off without them. In a weak moment, under the influence of drugs or alcohol, someone who is depressed may view suicide as a way out of their pain.

Recently, a distraught middle-aged woman came to my office for a mediumship session. Immediately I saw clairvoyantly the spirit of a young man, about 18 or 19, sit down next to her on the green sofa. He seemed very bright but disturbed; next, a feeling of loneliness. I couldn't quite place the feeling. Drugs? Schizophrenia? In this haze I saw the young man seek out a quiet corner of his college campus where he strung a rope over the rafters and hung himself. As he looked down at his lifeless body, he seemed amazed to still be alive.

Clairaudiently I heard, "Andrew." "Do you know an Andrew?" I asked the sitter. "Yes, she said tearfully, "he was my son. He committed suicide last month." "Andrew is here," I said. "He wants you to know he is sorry. He didn't mean to do it. He was just so very sad." A chill went through my body as I felt Andrew's deep regret. He knew now that he had thrown away his most precious possession, his life.

While death when it is our time can be a reunion with loved ones, those who die through suicide and homicide need special prayers to help them adjust. There are hospitals on the other side staffed with compassionate spirit doctors and therapists who work with these souls. But it takes time and the deceased must be ready to accept spiritual assistance.

Sometimes a soul is more than ready to meet their loved ones, but medical science interferes. I learned this through astral travel. One night when I was journeying out of my body, I stopped at a huge stadium where people were gathered. Since they did not seem too happy, I inquired "What is wrong?" A gray-haired woman answered, "We are all waiting to die, but we are stuck. We can't pass over because we are on life support." These souls were angry, because they wanted to on, but they had to bide their time until they could enter God's other door, death.

End Notes

1. Jenny Randles and Peter Hough, *Life After Death and the World Beyond.*

Suggested Reading

Atwater, P.M.H., *Coming Back to Life* and *Complete Idiot's Guide to the Near-Death Experience*

George Anderson, *We Don't Die*

E. A. Wallis Budge, *The Book of the Dead*

H. P. Blavatsky, *The Secret Doctrine*

Damion Brinkley, *Saved by the Light*

Hugh Lynn Cayce and Edgar Cayce, *No Death: God's Other Door*

Christopher Dunn, *The Giza Power Plant*

Betty Eadie, *Embraced by the Light*

Geoffrey Hodson, *Through the Gateway of Death*

Dr. Elisabeth Kübler-Ross, *The Wheel of Life*

Stephen Levine, *Who Dies?*

Dr. Raymond Moody, *Life After Life* and *Reunions*

Howard Murphet, *Beyond Death: The Undiscovered Country*

Carol E. Parrish-Harra, *Messengers of Hope*

Violet M. Shelley, *Reincarnation Unnecessary*

Jenny Randles and Peter Hough, *Life After Death and the World Beyond*

Dr. Kenneth Ring, *The Omega Project*

Tom Shroder, *Old Souls*

Dr. Ian Stevenson, *Twenty Cases Suggestive of Reincarnation*

John White, *A Practical Guide to Death and Dying*

Contacting Loved Ones

While it is gratifying to make contact with your loved ones through a medium, you don't really need an intermediary. The most common way spirit communicates with those on this side of life is through dreams. Take a moment each morning to write your dreams down. Date them and underline the names of departed loved ones who are in the dream. As you become more and more aware of your dreams, you will see how thin the veil between the two worlds really is.

Paramahansa Yogananda.

Chapter Three

Meditation

Work for god, love god alone, and be wise with god. When an
ordinary man puts the necessary time and enthusiasm into
meditation and prayer, he becomes a divine man.

—Paramahansa Yogananda

S TUDENTS OFTEN ASK ME "What is the best way to tune into the other side?" My advice: Meditation. With a focus on music, candle or breath, and a receptive attitude, most people can tune into inner peace and the other side.

When I first began meditating, I chose to use the candle meditation at the end of this chapter. After gazing into the flame of the candle, I would close my eyes and focus on the after image. At first, the image would wander, but with some practice I managed to keep it still.

After a month of daily practice sessions, I entered a different world. At first, I saw a sea of spirits who all seemed to be reaching out to me. This was the borderland or astral world where souls go upon death. I knew there were higher regions from my reading of Edgar Cayce, who instructed meditators not to stop at the lower astral level, but to go higher. Determined to reach the higher realms, I will my spirit to go up and over the multitude of spirits seeking contact. Soon, I was in bright, more peaceful place on the other side. Two people were patiently waiting for me. One was an elderly gentleman in a wheelchair and the other, a small lady holding a purple flower. "That's my name." she said. The couple turned out to be my great-grandfather and his housekeeper Violet.

With regular practice, more evidential meditations followed. After a few months, I discarded the candle technique and simply took a few deep breaths to entered trance. One event that stands out was a meditation in which I found myself in a limestone sarcophagus. It was so vivid that I could feel the cool limestone against my skin as an Egyptian high priest put the lid on the sarcophagus. I breathed down, as I had been taught to do and entered another world. Apparently, I had had a past life as a female initiate in ancient Egypt. About this time an Egyptian guide entered my life. His handsome face has been a reassuring presence in my life.

As I began to meditate in earnest, I was drawn to the Eastern literature, particularly the writings of Paramahansa Yogananda. As a young man, Yogananda was invited to the United States as a delegate to the 1920 International Congress of Religious Studies in Boston. With no funds and little knowledge of English, he relied on faith as his guide. Yogananda was astounded the following day when his thrifty father handed him a generous check, saying, "I give you this money not in the role of father but as a faithful disciple of Lahiri Mahasaya." More miracles followed when the Master Babaji materialized in the garb of a renunciate, with the advice, "Our Heavenly Father has heard your prayers. He commands me to tell you: Follow the behest of your guru and go to America. Fear not. You will be protected." The final miracle occurred aboard ship. While meditating en route to Boston, Yogananda remembered a lifetime in which he spoke English. Secure in the knowledge of his previous life as William the Conqueror and the grace of his guru, Yogananda delivered a forty-five minute lecture in "stirring and correct English."

Five years later, Yogananda established the Self-Realization Fellowship in Los Angeles, California. The organization remains active today, teaching kriya yoga, the union with the infinite through certain actions or rites (kriyas). While kriya yoga is only available to students of the Self-Realization Fellowship, Yogananda's lectures are published in *The Divine Romance*. In his lecture on "How You Can Approach God," Yogananda stresses morality: "Don't steal, don't lie, don't kill, don't commit adultery, don't commit any evil act." He then advises: "Be sincere, truthful, love your fellow man, practice introspection and self control." Only then is the student ready for meditation.[1]

On March 7, 1952, Yogananda entered *mahasamadhi* (a yogi's final conscious exit from the body) while he was giving a speech in honor of the Indian ambassador. Miraculous even in death, Yogananda requested that his body remain untouched for twenty days. Morticians at the Forest Lawn Cemetery were amazed to find that "no odor of decay emanated from the body at any time." The physical appearance of Yogananda's body on March 27, just before the bronze casket was put into position, was the same as it had been on March 7.[2]

Edgar Cayce, a Western mystic, also recommended spiritual seekers spend time in nature, prayer and meditation. The sleeping prophet also devoted his life to spiritual development, using Christ as a model. Cayce's guides firmly recommended a positive attitude, prayer, affirmation, and meditation. Cayce possessed the rare ability, when in trance, to tune into the wisdom found in the akashic records. Cayce's guide, the Source, stated: "Ye must learn to meditate as ye have learned to walk, to talk, to do any physical attributes of the mind (with relations to) the face, the attitudes, the conditions, the environs, of thy daily surroundings."

As a young bride, Elsie Sechrist was given less than a year to live, due to a heart condition. Edgar Cayce not only cured her, but also stimulated a lifelong interest. Her book, *Meditation: Gateway to Light*, recommends the Edgar Cayce approach of sincerity, enthusiasm and perseverance as keys to med-

itation. Once the spiritual aspirant has established a quiet space and a loving attitude she suggested: " One of our first tasks is to search our hearts
and minds, removing as as far as possible all resentment and hate and negative feelings." Then as Cayce suggested, a spiritual ideal should be established:

> Ideals are set from spiritual purposes, spiritual aspirations,
> desires, and there is a pattern in Him who is the way, the
> truth, and the light, and when that pattern is set according
> to such judgments, we find there is never the condemning
> of another. Because others do not agree with thee, condemn
> them not. For that what judgment is mete is measured to
> thee again. These ye find as the greater the problems in the
> present relationship with others. Then analyze first thyself
> and then ideals.—Edgar Cayce reading 5355-1

Once the ideal is established, mental and spiritual preparation as well
as patience is needed. According to Elsie Sechrist: "For most of us there will
follow a waiting period. The movement and expansion of the soul to a higher vibration of awareness is taking place at the unconscious level."[3] Thus,
while little is taking place in the outer world, much is going on in the inner
or spiritual world. Patience then becomes an active process one, which can
redirect and refine the soul.

During the actual process of meditation, the life force is raised from the
base of the spine to the upper chakras of the heart, throat, brow and crown.
Each of the chakras links with one of the endocrine glands. Elsie Sechrist
explains the glands of the three upper chakras thyroid, pineal and pituitary
become the most vital for meditation:

> The more materialistic we are, the denser we are spiritual-
> ly. Through prayer, meditation, right thinking and right
> eating, the body, the mind, the spirit become lighter and

more receptive to the spiritual atmosphere. We begin to perceive new and distant horizons. The fog of materialism has lifted and ESP is free to manifest itself. According to the readings [of Edgar Cayce], the thyroid is one of the three most spiritual centers in the body.[4]

Next, the pineal and pituitary glands are important for meditation. The pineal gland, which Sechrist terms the "Mind of Christ" is responsible for spiritual vision. As purification of the spiritual body takes place, the benefits are many. According to Sechrist, "As this center (the pituitary gland) becomes more and more purified, healing by the laying on of hands becomes possible. Healing through the power of the spoken word may also be effected for this purification makes possible fulfillment of an exalted purpose."[5]

Healers are advised to purify their own body and commit to a higher more spiritual purpose, if they wish to do laying on of the hands healing or spiritual counseling. Meditation is one key to opening the higher centers for creativity, clairvoyance and healing. Alice Bailey, who channeled *Discipleship in the New Age* gave meditation instructions for both individuals and groups who wish to progress. Her guide, known as the Tibetan, advised his students to put aside time for a structured meditation:

> I am going to ask you to give two relatively brief periods of time each day to a definite and defined meditation. One period (the most important) must be given to general group mediation, and the other to that meditation which I feel will enable you to function as an integrated personality, fused and blended in the consciousness of the soul. This will lead the group as a whole to function correctly, because of the individual group units are aligned and rightly adjusted.[6]

Through conscious meditation on the various energy centers or chakras, each student worked on opening and aligning the centers for greater spiritual work. Explaining "energy follows thought," the group was given the following invocation to use:

The Great Invocation
From the point of Light within the Mind of God
Let Light stream forth into the minds of men.
Let light descend on Earth.

From the point of Love within the Heart of God
Let Love stream forth into the hearts of men.
May Christ return to Earth.

From the center where the Will of God is known
Let purpose guide the little wills of men—
The purpose which the Masters know and serve.

Let the plan of Love and Light work out
And may it seal the door where evil dwells.
Let Light, Love, and Power restore the Plan on Earth.

Group meditation is very powerful.

Kryron, the guide of Lee Carroll, states the power of the group can be measured by taking that number of participants to the third power. For example, a group of twelve would have the power equivalent of 12 x 12 x 12 or 3,024 men. No wonder Edgar Cayce's sources said that if only twelve men had dedicated their thoughts sincerely toward peace, World War II could have been avoided!

Whether meditating in a group or alone, the process is the same. Sit or lie down so the spine is straight. Then focus all attention on one point. A device such as music, a mantra or even the breath can be used as the focal point. The brain will begin to relax, going from beta waves to alpha waves. With even more practice and spiritual intent, meditators go into a deeper trance. or theta waves. Meditation not only changes the brain waves of the body, it can affect the vital functions of the body, such as blood pressure and temperature.

Some New Age thinkers, such as Gregg Braden, believe spiritual practices like meditation can even change DNA. Others, such as Dr. Herbert Benson recommend meditation to lower blood pressure and prevent hypertension. Dr. Benson observed Tibetan monks able to withstand freezing temperatures while meditating all night in light robes without apparent discomfort. Instead of frost on their robes, a light steam appeared!

In *The Tibetan Book of Mental Development*, first-year monks are taught that "enthusiastic perseverance should be like stream, study and practice without break." Citing laziness and forgetfulness as obstacles to meditation, the Tibetan guidebook advises a quiet place, full instructions before retreating, and a meditation teacher to guide the student. Mental agitation, excessive sensuality and negative spirits living and dead should be avoided, if the student wishes to progress on the spiritual path.

The monks begin with simple meditations like focusing on a mantra or a mandala. This is known as "meditation with seed" in the East. Westerners tend to use this method exclusively, listening to music tapes of Kitaro's *Silk Road*, Marcey's *Inward Harmony* or a mantra such as *Om Namah Shivaya:* or the eternal sound of *Om*. With more experience, the monks no longer require "seed" meditation and can go into a deep state of meditation with simply a few breaths.

What actually happens in meditation? As the physical body becomes more relaxed, the astral body can detach. In the astral body, the meditator is now freed to make contact with loved ones, guides and angels. With sincerity and effort, the meditator may journey to higher planes—the higher mental plane, the Buddhic plane and finally Nirvana, or cosmic consciousness.

While few reach Nirvana, there are many other benefits of meditation. Dr. Deepak Chopra, in his book *Ageless Body, Timeless Mind*, shows how illnesses and the aging process can be slowed down by meditation. An other expert, Prof. Robert Ellwood, author of *Finding the Quiet the Mind*, found meditation helped students relieve the stresses of college life. Some meditators report feeling more peaceful, while others achieve mental clarity and find they can make decisions with greater clarity. Some even experience visual or auditory sensations—see vivid colors or hear heavenly sounds. Often at this point, the spiritual aspirant will make contact with a guide, such as an American Indian, Christian monk or nun or a Hindu master. The final benefit of meditation is that of "Moksha," or liberation from rebirth. While Moksha may take years of sincere practice, it is considered to be the highest achievement while in the body.

If you wish to experience the benefits of meditation, set aside a regular time and place for your inward journey. Then begin with a prayer of protection or simply surround yourself with white light. The yogis use a meditation cushion or rug to buffer themselves against unwanted earthly influences lingering on the ground. These unwanted influences may range from disturbances to the electrical field of the body to actual spirit possession.

Dr. Robert Becker in his book *Crosscurrents* details the many negative electrical forces, such as transformers, that can be disruptive to the human electromagnetic field. Even more disturbing are negative thought patterns and unsettled spirits of the dead. Both Dr. Edith Fiori and Dr Samuel Sagan have written books on the dangers of spirit possession. According to Dr. Sagan's book *Entity Possession*, unhappy spirits always want something whether it is food, sex, alcohol, drugs or power. Without taking some basic precautions, a spiritual aspirant may invite an unwanted guest.

Well aware of these dangers, Judy Hall five many suggestions for protection in her book, *The Art of Psychic Protection*. One technique that is easy to follow is the "light shower":

> Imagine a shower of light coming down from a point above
> your head. This light is cleansing and reenergizing. Let the

light wash away anything you have picked up that you need to release as the light passes through your aura. Then let the light recharge your aura.[7]

This exercise may be simplified by imagining yourself surrounded by a brilliant white light.

Next, decide on a regular time and place for meditation, preferably in the morning. For best results, the same time and space should be used. Think of this as a spiritual commitment. Just as guides make a commitment to be with the seeker, so the aspirant must be diligent about keeping the appointment. Start with five minutes of meditation practice and gradually, over a period of three months, lengthen to twenty minutes a session. Then choose a mental device, a music cd, mantra or mandala for focus. Whether the goal is relaxation, mental clarity, contact with a guide or liberation from rebirth, the following techniques yield universal benefits.

End Notes

1. Paramahansa Yogananda, *The Divine Romance, p. 364*

2. Paramahansa Yogananda, *Autobiography of a Yogi, p. 570*

3.Elsie Sechrist, *Meditation: Gateway to Light, p. 8*

4. Elsie Sechrist, *Meditation: Gateway to Light, p. 26*

5. Elsie Sechrist, *Meditation: Gateway to Light, p. 28*

6. Alice Bailey, *Discipleship in the New Age, Volume II, p. 7*

7. Judy Hall, *The Art of Psychic Protection, p. 137*

Healing Meditation

Sit in a comfortable position either on the floor or in a chair. Keep your spine straight. Focus on the breath. Visualize white light coming into your lungs as you take a deep breath through your nose. Then visualize stale negative energy leaving the body as you exhale through the mouth. Do this slowly seven times.

Next, visualize your lungs as upper, middle and lower regions. Breathe deeply and fill the bottom, middle and finally the upper portions of the lungs. Hold the air in for a count of five, at first. Over a period of time, practice until you can hold until a count of thirty.

Finish the session by surrounding your whole body with brilliant white light. The breath energy, or prana, can be stored for healing. As you hold the breath, the energy will become more concentrated. You may feel energy in your solar plexus or the palms of your hands may tingle. Now send this healing energy to any part of your body that is in need. With daily practice, your healing ability can progress to the point of helping others with hands-on healing techniques.

Guidance Meditation

Place a pen and a notebook at your side. You may have someone read these instruction to you in a quiet place, or the instructions may be recorded and played back.

See yourself in your favorite place to relax. This may be the beach or your own backyard. Visualize every detail of the place—sight, sound, touch, even the taste. You are totally relaxed. Very, very relaxed. (Pause.)

See white light shining above your head and gently coming down over your face, shoulder, chest, arms, hips, legs and feet. You are surrounded by brilliant protective white light. In a moment, at the count of three, your guide will join you. One you are relaxed. Two, you are excited about seeing your guide. On the count of three, but not before, you will make contact with your guide. Three your guide is right in front of you to lead the way. See or feel every detail of your guide. Take a moment to tune in. What does your guide look like? (Pause.)

Does the guide have a name or symbol to give to you? (Pause.)

Your guide has a message for you, a very important message. Take the next three minutes to tune into this message, which will help you at this time in your journey here on the earth plane. (Pause.)

Now that you have received the guidance, thank the guide for his/her loving-kindness. Gently wave good-bye. On the count of five, you will awaken and remember every detail of your session. You will be able to write all the details clearly and easily. The more you write, the more you remember.

One: You are rested.

Two: You are beginning to wake up.

Three: You will remember all details of your guide's message to you.

Four: You are alert. You feel energy in your body.

Five: You are fully awake, eyes wide open.

Suggested Reading

Dr. Herbert Benson, *The Relaxation Response*

Dr. Deepak Chopra, *Ageless Body, Timeless Mind*

Prema Chodron, *When Things Fall Apart*

John Coleman, *Quiet Mind*

Dr. Robert Ellwood, *Finding the Quiet Mind*

Harry Glover, *Meditation: The Light from Within*

Judy Hall, *The Art of Psychic Protection*

B. K. S. Iyengar, *Light on Yoga*

Jon Kabat-Zinn, *Wherever You Go, There You Are*

Howard Murphet, *Sai Baba: Man of Miracles*

Meredith Ann Puryear, *Healing Through Meditation and Prayer*

Henry Reed, *Your Mind: Unlocking Your Hidden Powers*

Dr. Samuel Sagan, *Entity Possession*

Elsie Sechrist, *Meditation: Gateway to Light*

Baird T. Spalding, *Life and Teaching of the Masters of the Far East*

Kevin Todeschi, *Edgar Cayce on the Akashic Records*

Paramahansa Yogananda, *Autobiography of a Yogi, The Divine Romance*

Bhante Wimala, *Lessons of the Lotus*

Chapter Four

Guides

A master never commands, never demands.

—Rev. Gladys Custance

MEDITATION IS AN IMPORTANT first step in mediumship because it puts students in touch with their guides who play a vital role in the development of mediumship. Guides have the power to see life from a higher perspective—much a helicopter pilot giving the traffic report to those below. The traveler then has the free will to choose his or her course. Master guides have great respect for free will. As Rev. Gladys Custance impressed upon her students, "A master never commands, never demands."

Gladys Custance and I were born with the gift of clairvoyance. While I met my first guide, a Hindu, in my crib, others quickly followed as I evolved. Some, such as my Egyptian master, came in meditation, others in dreams. That is how the deceased writer, Jack Kerouac, entered my life in1990. One night, I had a lucid dream in which I saw him dressed in the stripped robes of an Essene. Kerouac encouraged me in my writing efforts, stating emphatically, "Fame is on your horizon." Since then I have written three books, t wo of which, *Connecticut Ghosts* and *Séance 101* have been published by Schiffer Publishing Group.

There was more to the dream though. The spirit of Kerouac telepathically explained we had known each other as Essenes. He too had been interested in the work of Edgar Cayce. I was later able to verify this facet when I read Carolyn Cassidy's 1991 book, *Off the Road*:

> In 1956 an event took place that surprised and delighted us. A book named *The Search for Bridey Murphy* was published, and it caused a furor because it supported the evidence for reincarnation. To us it was perplexing that this book should receive so much attention, rather than a book such as *Many Mansions* written by modern scientists.[1]

They shared *Many Mansions,* an account of Edgar Cayce's readings on reincarnation, with their friend, Jack Kerouac, who mentioned to Carolyn Cassidy that he believed he felt his chronic phlebitis could be the result of his cruelties as a football player in his youth.

Many other writers have also been inspired by dreams, such as Charles Dickens, Graham Greene, and Jules Verne. Dickens received plots, characters, and names in dreams. Coleridge dreamed verbatim his poem, "Kubla Khan." However, he awoke before he received the last lines and was never able to finish the poem. Graham Greene's widow, Vivien, revealed that some of his novels were inspired by dreams. Science fiction writer Jules Verne was also inspired by dreams, while Kerouac wrote a whole book based on dreams, *The Book of Dreams.* His dreams also provided material for his novels, *On the Road* and *The Dharma Bums.* Mark Twain not only received material in dreams, but he also met dead relatives and friends in dreams. He even foresaw his own brother's accidental death. In his *Notebook* he described conversations with "the living and dead, rational and irrational."

Mediumship is a common occurrence in dreams. Many people just like Mark Twain reported talking to their relatives in dreams. How is this possible? While the physical body is fast asleep, the sleeper can travel in his astral body to visit disincarnates who dwell in the astral plane and beyond. Often loved ones and guides will descend to the astral plane to aid in communication. Dr. Harmon Bro in *Edgar Cayce on Dreams* commented on spirit contact "Cayce confirmed that this (the dream) had been authentic contact, and warned again, as he had already told the dream, that to seek contact too often with a discarnate would bring distress to the discarnate, holding them back from their own full journey."[2] Still another, perhaps more helpful use of dreams, is that of reviewing past lives. "One of the 'dead' who still lives," said Cayce, "is the dreamer himself. In dreams he may see himself as he has been in other lives."[3]

Keeping a dream journal is an excellent way to tap into psychic material and to connect with guides. If you do start to keep a dream journal, you will be astonished by not only by the guides you meet but by the many déjà vu events that occur. Edgar Cayce said, "Nothing of importance occurs in our life that is not first previewed in dream." Here are some suggestions, it you wish to remember your dreams and connect with guides:

1. Before going to bed, place a notebook (a nice thick one) on your nightstand.

2. Give yourself the suggestion, "I will remember my dreams in every detail."

3. When you awake, write something in your dream journal even if it is only a fragment or feeling.

If you are unable to remember anything, try setting the alarm clock for the middle of your sleep cycle when you are more likely to hit Rapid Eye Movement or dream sleep. Another suggestion to induce dreaming is to wake up fully, then go back to bed for a while. Often you will drift into the light stage one sleep, the dream state, and you will remember a dream when you awaken from your "second" sleep. Once you have recorded the dream, save it for later in the day for more careful study. When you have more time, make a permanent record of your dreams in a journal.

While dreams are portals to the other side, so are mirrors. That is how I met the Rev. Arthur Ford. When I was invited to conduct the Official Houdini Séance in 1997 at the Goodspeed Opera House, I was undecided about accepting the invitation. I was about to decline, then quite unexpectedly, I made contact with the Reverend Ford who conducted the first Houdini Séance. It happened as I casually glanced into a mirror as I brushed my hair. Clairaudiently, I heard, "Houdini has a message for you." I sensed immediately that it was the voice of Arthur Ford, who had been a friend of my teachers Rev. Kenneth and Gladys Custance.

Many guides like the Rev. Arthur Ford come in to assist a medium's development, while some guides may only come in on a one-time basis during emergencies. Such was the case one cold, Connecticut evening. I had just driven into town to drop a letter off at the post office when I heard the dull thud of a flat tire. What to do? Should I walk the two miles home for help, or chance driving back? Before, I could decide, I felt the presence of our mechanic, "Mobile Ernie," who had died two months before. "Just drive slowly, Mrs. Kuzmeskus," Ernie's calm spirit instructed me. "You'll be okay." He gallantly sat beside me until I safely pulled into our driveway. When I turned to thank Ernie, he had disappeared. Guides like Ernie are there when we need them; then they move on.

Other guides have a more permanent place in my life, such as my personal Hindu guide. Ever since I can recall, I have seen guides. When I was in my crib, I would awaken to a brown face with the most magnetic eyes and white muslin turban. This Hindu guide seemed genuinely interested in me and would often answer my thoughts telepathically.

As a child, I simply accepted my Hindu guide. By the time I entered college, I sometimes just ignored guidance, much to my regret. For example, when I heard "Use the other dryer" at the Kenmore Square laundromat, I stubbornly kept putting my wet clothes into the dryer I had chosen along with all my change. When I turned the knob, the dryer did not turn on. Out of money, I had to carry a heavy load of wet wash back to my apartment.

Jack Kerouac, noted
American writer.

While guides can assist in everyday affairs, most come for spiritual purposes. For instance, I glimpsed the handsome face of my Egyptian guide as
I began to meditate regularly. Clairvoyantly, I saw man in his forties dressed
in white robes and a horizontally striped headdress with a cobra rising from
the middle of his forehead. Just looking into his magnetic brown eyes would
make me lightheaded. As I entered the silence, I sensed immediately that he
was a spiritual teacher and master clairvoyant —a fact confirmed in a reading with the Rev. Gladys Custance.

The Rev. Gladys Custance, by the way, also had a personal Hindu guide
known affectionately as "the Professor." When she taught her Friday night
class, Mrs. Custance would drift into trance and the comforting voice of the
Professor would take over. It wasn't long before students smelled the scent
of lilacs or saw clouds of ectoplasm, as well as the familiar blue and white
spirit lights. The Rev. Kenneth Custance's guide, a silver-haired Franciscan
monk dubbed "the Abbot" was also present to assist the group. While the
Custances had been acquainted with their guides for many years, many
group members were just getting to know their guides during meditation,.
Here, they would receive descriptions of the their guides through the
Professor as well as through their thoughts.

Mrs. Custance also made herself available for private sessions as well.
In one of these private sittings, she gave descriptions of several of my guides,
including my Hindu guide and the tall Egyptian, as well as an American
Indian who was a protector.

"His name is Yellow Jacket," Mrs. Custance pronounced. A stickler for
names, she was not happy until she got the spirit's names exact. For instance,
on one occasion my friend's uncle had passed over with an unusual nick-
name, "Peppy," said Gladys. Then turning toward the spirit she said, "That's
not right—Pepo; is there such a name?" As usual she was right; Uncle Pepo
had died the week before!

Mrs. Custance was, by the way, a full-trance medium. While her guide
was inclined toward philosophy, other mediums such as Margery Crandon

attracted more down-to-earth types. Crandon's guide was her deceased brother, Walter Stinson. who loved to come through his sister with a signature whistle and a few wisecracks. Walter's language could be salty, but he was sincere in proving his existence through many experiments. By the way, Margery Crandon was just as surprised as her husband, Dr. Crandon, when she turned out to be a natural trance medium.

While neither Walter Stinson or the Professor were famous, occasionally guides are well known when on the earth plane. For example, Andrew Jackson Davis had two famous guides, the Swedish clairvoyant Emmanuel Swedenborg and the Roman physician Galen.

> In 1844, Davis was suddenly overcome by some power which transported him to the Catskill Mountains (forty miles away). In this semi-trance state, he claims to have met the philosopher and Greek physician Galen and the Swedish seer Emanuel Swedenborg, both of whom had been dead for some time. He also experienced a great mental illumination at that time.[4]

Davis was known for his medical clairvoyance. He diagnosed and prescribed cures through spirit communication. and even became a physician so he could practice medicine. Davis was also a prodigious writer, channeling over twenty books and making detailed prophecies which included the discovery of the planets Neptune and Pluto. He also prophesied the birth of modern Spiritualism: "It is a truth that spirits commune with one another while one is in the body and the other in the higher spheres—and this, too, when the person in the body is unconscious of the influx, and hence cannot be convinced of the fact; and this truth will ere long present itself in the form of a living demonstration. And the world will hail with delight the ushering in that era when the interiors of men will be opened, and the spiritual communion will be established such as is now being enjoyed by the inhabitants of Mars, Jupiter, and Saturn!"[5]

Fifty years later Edgar Cayce began his work as a medical clairvoyant. His main guide was simply called the Source. Later, a medical doctor from the 1800s was identified as one of Cayce's guides, which explains why the medical readings are filled with Victorian prose and convoluted sentences. Occasionally even the archangels Gabriel and Michael came through the sleeping prophet.

Why such lofty guides? According to Cayce, "Mind is the builder." We attract guides by our attitude of service. Mediums have at least one main guide and several assistants—a master teacher, a chemist, and a personal guide. For instance, Andrew Jackson Davis had the spirit of the ancient physician Galen to help him with medical clairvoyance. Edgar Cayce's guide was simply called the Source. Paul Solomon, whose readings resembled Cayce's, also had a guide called the Source. Arthur Ford's guide was more personal—his childhood friend, Fletcher. In 1924, Fletcher came in as a life-long guide. Some trance mediums such as Eileen Garrett had several guides. Hers included Uvani, a fourteenth-century Arab soldier, and later Abdul Latif, a seventeenth-century Persian physician, who dealt mainly with healing, followed by Tahotah and Ramah, who claimed no earthy incarnations.

Often mediums first meet their guides through other mediums or while in trance. Medium James Van Praagh, who attended parochial schools run by the Sisters of Mercy, was told by clairvoyant Irene Martin-Giles that his guide was a nun from the Sisters of Mercy—Sister Theresa. Van Praagh was astounded by the details: "The clairvoyant described Sister Theresa in detail, right down to the brilliant blue color of her eyes." The clairvoyant, went on the give him a second guide: "Irene continued to tell me that a Chinese man named Chang was my spiritual teacher."[6] Sometimes spirit doctors such as "Doctor Harry Aldrich" come through Van Praagh's trance sessions, as well as an American Indian, Golden Feather.[7]

Sylvia Browne's guide is a South American Indian woman whom she dubbed Francine. Browne met her guide when she was eight. Her guide reassured her with these words: "Don't be afraid, Sylvia. I come from God."[8] Her psychic grandmother taught Sylvia early on not to be afraid of Francine. "She explained that we all have spirit guides who are assigned to us as helpers. The only difference was that she and I could see ours."[9]

Channeler Elwood Babbit met his guides as an adult. His main guide was Dr Fisher. However, on occasions, Mark Twain made an appearance, as well as Mahatma Gandhi. I was in the Boston Hotel ballroom when Gandhi came through. The energy was so charged after his message, no one could speak. After about five minutes, I broke the silence with the question that was on many people's minds: "What can we do to create world peace?" He then channeled an eloquent message on non-violence.

Another great medium I had the privilege to witness was the Brazilian healer known as John of God. His sole focus is healing, which he does without thought of payment. The guides who work through John of God are sprits of deceased doctors, such as Dr. Oswaldo Cruz, Dr. Augusto de Almeida, and Dr. Jose Valdivino. These guides perform psychic surgery, sometimes with the scalpel, more often through vibrational healing. John of God's most famous guide is the spirit of Saint Ignatius of Loyola, who founded the Jesuit order during the sixteenth century.

Every year in July on the on the anniversary of Saint Ignatius's birthday, there is a magnificent celebration at John of God's clinic at Casa de Dom Inácio de Loyola near Abadianaia, Brazil. My husband Ron and our friend Mary Arendt were at the Casa for the 2007 celebration. People attended from all over the world. The healing energy was extraordinary as Saint Ignatius incorporated for about twenty minutes.

Guides like John of God's are here to work solely for humanity. Many years ago, his guide Sister Rita told him "I will always be with you as long as you do not charge for healing." She is very much present at the Casa. I "met" Sister Rita on my second day there. She materialized and sat on the bed next to mine. She had come to comfort me when I was frustrated by the failure of the local ATM machine. She kindly told me—"I am sorry I cannot help you—you world has its rules and our world has its own." While,

I was temporarily short of cash, the loving presence of Saint Rita gave me peace of mind beyond price.

End Notes

1. Carolyn Cassidy, *Off the Road,* Penguin Books, New York, NY, 1991, page 277.
2. Harmon Bro, *Edgar Cayce on Dreams,* Paperback Library, New York, NY, 1968, page 81.
3. Harmon Bro, *Edgar Cayce on Dreams,* Paperback Library 1968, New York, NY, page 190.
4. *wwwandrewjacksondavis.com*
5. *www.spiritwritings.com/andrewjacksondavis*
6. James Van Praagh, *Talking to Heaven,* Penguin Books, New York, NY, 1997, page 46.
7. James Van Praagh, *Talking to Heaven,* Penguin Books, New York, NY, 1997, page 47.
8. Sylvia Browne and Antoinette May, *Adventures of a Psychic,* Hay House, Carlsbad CA, 1990, page 6.
9. Sylvia Browne and Antoinette May, *Adventures of a Psychic,* Hay House, Carlsbad CA, 1990, page 6.

Suggested Reading

Andrews, Ted, *How to Meet and Work with Spirit Guides*
Browne, Sylvia, *Contacting Your Spirit Guide*
Chaney, Robert, *Mediums and Their Development*
Eynden, Rose Vanden, *So You Want to Be a Medium: A Down to Earth Guide*

Chapter Five

Spiritualist Circle

Our lives are shaped not as much by our experience, as by our expectations —George Bernard Shaw

Y THE TIME I ENCOUNTERED Saint Rita in 2007, I had been a certified medium for thirty-five years and was not surprised by the presence of spirit. My training began in a Boston Spiritualist circle presided over by the Rev. Gladys Custance and her husband the Rev. Kenneth Custance. Both were veteran mediums and ministers ordained by the National Association of Spiritualist Churches. The NASC defines Spiritualism as "the Science, Philosophy, and Religion of continuous life, based upon the demonstrated fact of communication, by means of mediumship, with those who live in the Spirit World."

While both the Rev. Kenneth Custance and his wife, the Rev. Gladys Custance, were ardent Spiritualists, they did not start out as mediums— both had been professional musicians. In fact, they met through music in the 1920s when they were on the same bill. When the twenty-five-year-old Gladys met twenty-two-year-old Kenneth, she didn't view him as a suitor: "I wasn't interested in Kenneth when we first met—I thought he was too young." However, it wasn't long before she noted the twinkle in Kenneth's eye.

After they married, Kenneth came to appreciate another talent of Gladys—her psychic ability. Many times, when Kenneth was busy earning a living as a music teacher, he would send the bereaved to his wife for comfort. It wasn't long before Gladys was as busy as medium as she was as a harpist. Soon, they became involved with Spiritualism and they took correspondence courses offered by the NASC.

They devoted as much time as they could to serving the First Spiritualist Church of Onset, Massachusetts, which they founded. They also maintained a private circle in Boston. Every Friday evening, they made the commute from their home on the Cape to Boston to conduct the circle. In 1969, their Boston group had expanded, to about forty sitters, including several teachers, a rabbi, and two MIT professors. One of the professors proudly told the group how he believed in the 1940s that the United States would have a man on moon. When his colleagues expressed skepticism, he pounded his desk declaring, "In twenty-five years, I'll have a piece of moon on my desk!" In 1969 the prediction came true and one of the astronauts brought back a moon rock as a gift to the professor.

Another talented member of our group was Ida Donadio, a psychic homemaker from Medford, Massachusetts. While Ida was always perceptive, she tended to second guess herself. She always seemed surprised when the members of the group reassured her with, "You are right on, Ida." When this modest medium graduated from the group, she founded the Medford Spiritualist Church.

In contrast, Marion Proctor, a well-known figure skater, seemed the picture of confidence. She was well educated, a graduate of Wheelock College in Boston, and was active as a figure-skating instructor in Bourne and Boston. Occasionally, spirits of the Olympic athletes she had trained and who had passed over in a plane crash made an appearance in the circle. Generous with her time, she often served as hostess for the Custances,

My favorite member of the group was an attractive woman in her forties-Florence. She had been a model and a professional opera singer-she also had a ghost in her suburban Boston home. Apparently, the original owner, who had committed suicide in the pantry, was still not at peace. Eventually the Custances performed an exorcism on the house, much to Florence's peace of mind.

Each member of the group had his or her own story to tell. There seemed to be a wonderful blend of energy present. This is important, as even one negative sitter can have a deleterious effect. The Custances made sure they ran a tight ship. For starters, a new member had to wait to be invited to attend the home circle. It was usually suggested you attend a meeting or two. When both felt you might be right for the group, you were invited to join the circle. If later on there was any serious moral misconduct, you were dismissed. To my knowledge only a few members were reprimanded—one a lonely middle-aged secretary who like to play "footsie" with men in the darkness was told in no uncertain terms to keep her feet to herself. She did and remained a member. However, a foursome of a married writer, his wife, and two men in their twenties all were dismissed when it was discovered that the husband's "sons" were actually his lovers.

Most of the people in the Friday night group accepted criticism of either minister as being for their benefit. After all, Gladys Custance had taken her share of feedback from the Professor, who was very active in Gladys's development. At one point, he insisted she not do any reading for a year, recommending that all information be given inspirationally!

The Reverend Custance gave her students three tips on mediumship. One: "Tension shuts the door." Often affirmations and prayers were said to ease the fears of those in need. A much-repeated affirmation was: "A mighty God force goes before me— making easy, instant, and perfect my way." In order to lighten the atmosphere, Kenneth Custance usually opened the circle with an anecdote or two. These stories were followed by the group singing verses such as "God is Love," to the tune of "Silent Night".

We would then take a break. After the break, Mrs. Custance's second rule came into play. "Give impressions as they come to you," The group sat for an hour in complete silence in the living room of the spacious Commonwealth Avenue apartment. Mrs. Custance believed in giving just the impression, and allowing spirit to make any additional comments. A typical impression: "I have someone here with the name Richard." A sitter might answer, "Yes, that's the name of my husband who passed over last year." Then once Mrs. Custance had the voice of the sitter, she would continue the message from spirit. That's because spirit works off voice vibration.

Then the lights were turned off and the spirits did their work. Often smells of lilacs, roses, and cherry tobacco would permeate the room as different spirits made their appearances. Almost everyone experienced a heaviness much like a helmet as the healing energies worked to open the crown chakras and third eyes of fledgling clairvoyants.

Toward the end of the evening session, the energy would shift. After all the messages were given for the evening, Mrs. Custance would say, "Did anyone feel a change of forces?" This indicated that the energy was going down as the spirits departed for the evening. It is hard to explain, It just seems like a "dead zone"—no lights, energy or fragrance remained after the spirits departed.

While students were honing their mediumship skills, they were also encouraged to work on their characters—Mrs. Custance's third tip. She always insisted on high standards for behavior and dress. As a professional harpist, she knew the importance of appearances on stage. And she gave attention to the details that make a performance perfect. For instance, when another medium was scheduled to share the stage with her, Mrs. Custance unfailingly called ahead to inquire what the medium was planning to wear so she could coordinate her wardrobe for a unified effect on stage.

The Rev. Gladys Custance was very much respected in her field and eventually trained fifty professional mediums. She was also very professional when it came to clients, keeping confidences and respecting the territories of other mediums. Once when a client of Arthur Ford asked for a reading, she refused until the Reverend Ford agreed to the session, which he readily did.

Arthur Ford maintained a home at Camp Lily Dale in Cassadaga, New York. The camp is part of the National Association of Spiritualist Churches. The NASC is the largest and oldest Spiritualist association in the United States. This organization hands out two types of certificates for mediumship—physical and mental. The former is most unusual today, because most mediums receive mental mediumship certificates.

The Custances also served at Lily Dale. They both enjoyed travel and took students to Camp Chesterfield in Indiana in the 1950s. Here they witnessed slate séances. Each participant was given two small slates with a piece of chalk placed between the two slates. The slates were then securely bound with twine and placed in the middle of the table. While the sitters sat holding hands and singing, sounds of chalk scratching were heard. When the scratching stopped, the sitters untied their slates. All received messages written by spirit. Celeste and her mother, a widow who had just lost her physician husband, received a chalk message written in the doctor's own handwriting.

It was at Camp Chesterfield that Gladys was amazed to meet the spirit of her deceased grandmother. Her spirit fully materialized in the séance room, and even offered to play a song on Gladys's harp. When grandmother asked, "What do you want me to play, dear?" Gladys quickly replied, "Our favorite song."

"When the spirit played Brahms' Lullaby, I knew she was Grandmother. That is the song we played every night before bedtime," Mrs. Custance told the enraptured group.

Kenneth Custance also had his stories to tell. He had had many encounters with spirits and was especially interested in apports, materialized objects. He maintained a collection of twenty or more apports that he and Gladys had collected in their travels. Each had a unique story. One woman, who had lost a stone in her ring while gardening, was surprised to receive the same stone as an apport from spirit. The stone had been teleported via the medium's trumpet. Often sitters were not to touch the objects that came from the trumpet for a few minutes, because they were still warm and not quite solid yet.

Most talented mediums like Edgar Cayce are born with the gift. However, as with any other talent, it needs to be nurtured. When it is not nurtured, the gift can disappear, as it did in the case of one of Cayce's last clients—Faith Harding, known as "the Little Prophetess." According to Cayce, she was the incarnation of Saint Cecilia, a fact not accepted by her dogmatic father, Harry Harding. When he won custody of Faith and her siblings in a bitter divorce, he curtailed all psychic contact, even keeping the child from her spiritual, devoted mother, Virginia Harding.

According to Sidney Kirkpatrick, who interviewed Faith more recently, she had no memory of the "Little Prophetess." Apparently, gifts of spirit like other talents can be nurtured or destroyed. Even in Faith Harding's life reading, Edgar Cayce had warned the parents. The Source admonished Faith's parents and those around her to nurture her in the "spirit of truth" to provide her with love, kindness, and gentleness of spirit in those things that bring "constructive, hopeful, helpful forces into the experiences of others" and not to let her experience distrust, envy, malice, or jealousy.

Edgar Cayce, who believed the psychic to be of the soul, constantly sought and obtained guidance from spiritual forces he called the Source. He was undoubtedly the greatest trance medium of his time. Others have followed in his footsteps with varying degree of success. Modern channelers include J. Z. Knight of Ramtha fame, Jach Pursel who channels Lazaris, and the late Paul Solomon, who channeled the Source, similar to Edgar Cayce. Elwood Babbitt's main guide was Dr. Fisher, but he also channeled Mark Twain. Babbitt wrote several books based on channeled sources: *Talks With Christ, Vishnu in God Within,* and *Perfect Health.*

Most of today's mediums are mental mediums: Sylvia Browne, Jonathan

Edwards, George Anderson, and James Van Praagh. The media has done much to promote their talents. Sylvia Browne was an unknown until she appeared on the *Montel Williams Show*, as was James Van Praagh until he made an appearance on CNN's *Larry King Live* to promote his book, *Talking to Heaven*. Jonathan Edwards now has his own program, *Crossing Over*.

With the renewed interest in mediumship, the formal séance is back in style. A formal séance is usually limited to twelve participants seated around a table. The room should be as quiet as possible, with the telephone disconnected. Put a tape recorder with fresh batteries in the center of the table to record messages. A glass of water should be placed in front of the medium and each of the sitters. The water will act as a conductor for psychic energy, as well as a thirst quencher. Once the medium has a established rapport, the séance can begin with a phrase such as, "Spirit, do you have any messages for us?"

Wait patiently for spirit to come through the medium. As Larry Dweller cautions in *The Beginner's Guide to Mediumship*, "Don't be impatient for contact. It will either flow or won't flow." Let the sitters know beforehand: spirit contact takes time. Many participants report that they feel a change of energy or a charged atmosphere at this point. Dweller points out: "Remember two very important things: the spirits of the departed are everywhere in the parallel dimensions (astral plane and higher planes), and the only reality spirits have in our own dimension is what we give them. By the intensity of our vibration level for reception, our intense faith, we draw them near to us."

When I do a channeling session, I always tape it, as I like to identify the spirits present after I come out of trance. Never be afraid to test the spirit. Spirit usually will try to bring through information no one else would know or information that can be verified. For example, late one winter evening in 2002, I paused from working on an astrology book in progress, *Soul Cycles*. I felt the presence of Boston astrologer Marcia Moore, who had died a few years earlier. Marcia, a writer herself, was very cordial and encouraging. I was surprised when I heard her spirit say, "I was also interested in Sai Baba." Since I had never read anything in her books about Sai Baba, I questioned the statement in my mind. Marcia simply said, "Check my book." I looked at the index of her last book, *Journeys into the Bright World,* and sure enough, Sai Baba's name was listed

Suggested Reading

Buckland, Raymond, *Doors to Other Worlds*
Chaney, Robert G., *Mediums and the Development of Mediumship*
Edwards, Harry, *A Guide for the Development of Mediumship*
Hurst, Brian, *Heaven Can Help*
Owens, Elizabeth, *Spiritualism and Clairvoyance for Beginners*
Smith, Gordon, *Developing Mediumship*

The Rev. Gladys Custance and the Rev. Kenneth Custance.

Chapter Six

Psychometry

The softest thing in the universe overcomes the hardest thing in the universe. That without substance can enter where there is no room. Hence, I know the value of non-action. Teaching without words and work without doing are understood by very few.
                                                              —Lao Tzu

A FTER I HAD BEEN in the Friday circle about a year, the regulars seemed like lifelong friends. We always had so much to talk about. I was especially fond of a elegantly dressed, fifty-year-old lady, Mary Rogers, who took me under her wing. Mary had been with the Custances for about twenty years and was a trusted confidant who often helped out at the First Spiritualist Church in Onset, Connecticut. This suburban mother of three had devoted her life to spiritual studies and was well-read in occult literature. She was the first person I met when I joined the group and she remains the most gracious person I have ever encountered to this day. I was also in awe of Nelly, a close friend of the Custances who was a renowned concert harpist. In fact, she was so close to them that Gladys Custance used to quip, "Nelly even went on our honeymoon!" Apparently, the Custances combined their honeymoon travel with a trio harp performance.

Other sitters included a young married couple: Don, an insurance executive, and his high-strung wife, Karen. They routinely brought their five year old and put him to sleep in an adjoining room during the circle. Since they lived in the next town to me, I had the chance to visit with Karen when the group disbanded for winter and summer breaks. One evening, Karen told me about taking private lessons with Mrs. Custance.

"That sounds interesting," I said. "What do you do?"

"We do psychometry," she replied. "Professor comes in and teaches you how to tune into people by holding their rings or watches."

It wasn't long before I arranged monthly psychometry lessons with Mrs. Custance. During the first lesson, she gave me an antique ring to hold.

"Just relax, dear, and allow yourself to tune into the owner."

Soon, my head was filled with impressions. Tentatively, I began: "It belonged to an older woman—a relative of yours. She's been gone a while and sends her love." As these words poured out, Professor, who had now taken over Mrs. Custance's body, just nodded.

Professor was present at all my psychometry lessons. The séance room had a charge of energy that I could feel intensify as the Professor's spirit took control of the medium. As I became more accustomed to the energy present—which at times resembled the sacred silence of a cathedral—my readings improved. When the session was about to end, there was a perceptible drop in the energy. Professor would alert me by asking, "Do you have a last question?"

While psychometry was a new experience for me, it is not a new phenomenon. The word "psychometry" comes from two Greek words: *psyche*, which means soul, and *metry*, to measure. The term was coined in 1842 by Joseph R. Buchanan, who claimed it could be used to measure the soul of all things. He developed a theory that things have their own emanations that can be read by the psychic who holds them. Psychometric impressions may come in the form of feelings, impressions, sounds, scents, or even tastes.

The lessons I received from Mrs. Custance were invaluable She taught me to take a few deep breaths and just relax. Soon I was receiving impressions. Colors came in first. Then I might see an object that had personal meaning. For example, a blue Edgewood Tobacco can might indicate a cigar smoker or someone who chewed tobacco. After these preliminary exercises, I began to tune into the owner of the object.

"I see an older woman who wore her gray hair in a crown of braids on top of her hair," I would say to Professor. He would then acknowledge this was true and then probe for more details. For example, "What color are her eyes?" or "Can you sense how she passed?"

In a few months, I was giving a full ten-minute description of the deceased. And the once general messages became more specific. For instance, "I see a woman here with short white hair, quite simple in style, blue eyes and tiny build. She gives the name of Edith and says 'hello' to you. Edith says she never met Kenneth. She was a musician, not a harpist, but a pianist. It has been at least twenty years since she died of a heart condition. She looks about fifty."

Gladys would then say, "That's exactly right; I knew her before I married Kenneth."

Now I begin all my readings with holding a watch or ring. If a woman arrives without any jewelry, I will request her tube of lipstick or Chapstick, since it is an object that one doesn't share. For gentlemen without a watch, I ask if I may hold their wallet. If absolutely nothing is available to hold (which is rare), I have the sitter hold a piece of paper for a few minutes. I usually avoid keys unless I am sure the sitter never loans them out. Also antique jewelry can be tricky—the original owner may be the one to get the reading, not the sitter.

Once I have the object in my hands, I say a prayer of intention out loud: "Loving Father, Divine Mother, may that which is for the sitter's highest good come through. We know with our little will, little can be accomplished, but with God's will all things are possible."

Then I do three slow head rolls to the right and three to the left to release any tension in my neck. Next, I take seven deep breaths to relax. I always respect my client. It is not my place to judge an alternate lifestyle or a different religion. A psychometrist's job is just to give impressions accurately as they are received. For instance, if I sense an interest in mechanics and then see the face of an older man, I would state "I feel mechanical and see the face of an older man about seventy-five."

Often a client will interrupt: "That's my Dad—he was a mechanic!" When I hear a name, I might say, "I hear the name Georgie." (I was tempted to say, "He is here," but as Mrs. Custance taught, I just gave what I receive.)

"Oh," said the middle aged man in front of me, with tears streaming down his face, "that was my wife Georgina."

While physical descriptions and names are easy for the client to identify, sometimes a symbol may not be. For example, "I see a giraffe."

Client: "I don't know." Then I would interpret: "Since I often see a giraffe when a situation needs to be overlooked, I feel there is someone in your life right now, whom you need to overlook."

"That's exactly right," answered the blonde, forty-eight-year-old nurse in front of me. "I was ready to quit on Friday, but I can't. I have a son in college."

"Don't worry," I answered. "I see a three. In three weeks, things will be better at work—as long as you overlook the present situation."

All situations have options, so I always try to be encouraging and give the alternatives. For instance, one pretty, twenty-five-year-old, single mother of two asked about her future with her married boyfriend, who was also her landlord.

I answered, "He is not going to leave his wife. In three years you could find yourself out on the street. Spirit is encouraging you to move now."

"No way," she replied. "He's taking a hundred dollars off my rent."

When I pointed out that security was not a break in your rent, but your name on the deed, she was silent.

Of course, some people will try to hide information from the medium. On one occasion, I was doing a public demonstration of mediumship. Spirit pointed me toward a man in a blue shirt who looked about thirty.

"May I come to you?" I asked.

"Yes," he answered.

"A tall, older man is standing behind you, and he says 'You will pass the exam.'"

The impertinent sitter answered, "I am not taking any exam."

I asked spirit, "What exam?"

His grandfather replied from the other side, "The post office exam."

The man in the blue shirt stubbornly insisted, "You are wrong."

"Well, that is what spirit is telling me," I said, and was about to turn to another member of the audience, when the man pulled out some papers from his pocket.

"You're right," he grumbled. "These are the admission papers for the post office exam I am taking on Saturday." In cases of deception, I try to keep an even mind. "That's great," I said and moved on the next person.

While candor is sometimes needed, it is also important to be tactful and if possible keep a sense of humor. Instead of saying, "I sense the presence of man who was a drunk," I might temper the description with, "I have someone here who liked a drink or two—sometimes four or five gin and tonics!"

Often the client will give me some feedback. "That's my father—he was a good man but a drinker."

With patience, most people, even beginners, can pick up impressions from an object. Even beginners can be very accurate, as I found out after an especially busy day which included back-to-back classes at two community colleges and Hartford's rush-hour traffic. Since we began "Introduction to Parapsychology" class with psychometry exercises, I casually handed my wedding band to one of the ladies in the front row.

"Boy," she said, "do I feel dizzy, like I have been running in circles. I feel like I can't calm down."

I had to admit sheepishly, "That's right. It has been a hectic day and I was almost late for class."

Objects never lie. It just takes some patience and sensitivity to read them. Here are some suggestion to help develop psychometry abilities: First realize, psychometry is a natural ability and a safe way to tune in. You do not have to be a medium to use psychometry—just receptive to impressions. Start by choosing a quiet location without distractions. Take the object in your hands, preferably an object the sitter has worn and that has some significance. Start with a prayer of intention, either silently or aloud.

Relax with a few deep breaths. Be still for moment or two. Then, as images and impressions come in, give them out without editing them. This is crucial, as something that is trivial to the psychometrist may have great meaning to the sitter, either now or in the future. Once I told the father of a seriously ill three year old, "I feel an operation coming which has never been done before on a child. It may save her life."

Later the doctors in New Haven said these exact words to her father. "We would like to do an operation on your daughter which has never been done on a child, but which may save her life." The wording was the essential part of the message. as it gave the father the courage to go ahead with the procedure, which did save his daughter's life.

Also, some messages may be quite lengthy or detailed, but do not try to edit the information. Just let it flow. If, on the other hand, the information is vague, pause and give the sitter a moment to ask a follow-up question.

The client said, "John. I know three Johns and a Jack. Could it be my grandfather John?" When she said "grandfather," I saw a blue light over her head, so I knew it was the grandfather's spirit coming in.

Personally, I rarely give messages about death, as I believe death is in God's hands. However, if a client has a loved one who is ill, I may say, "It looks like three years or less" or, "I would try to see them soon." Sometimes "It looks like you may be taking time off in February" if I sense a passing that month.

As you progress with psychometry, you will find your own way to deliver disturbing news. Even my own guides try to deliver bad news with care. On March 4, I saw a vivid image of a red jack-in-the-box pop up as I was turning onto the highway on my way to work. Since red is the color of danger and a jack-in-the-box a symbol of surprise, I sensed immediately that an unpleasant surprise was coming. Two days later, March 6, I casually checked my messages at the end of my work day and heard, "Mrs. Kuzmeskus, this is Manor Care. Please call us immediately."

When I reached my mother's nurse, Alice, she said, "I am sorry to tell you—your mother passed away this morning in her sleep." Even though I had been praying for an easy death for my eighty-nine-year-old mother, I was stunned by the message.

Messages can have their happier moments too—when you see a new love or a child coming into someone's life. Once a psychic told my husband who had been out of work for some time, "I see you working at a part-time job which is a hobby." We were both stumped until a neighbor offered Ron a temporary job at his nursery; Ron's hobby is gardening.

Psychometry can also be especially helpful in locating lost objects. One widow came to me in distress because her two-caret diamond engagement ring was missing.

"Don't worry; it is safe," was the message from spirit. "You will find it in May."

Sure enough, when she went to put new flowers in the urns on her patio in May, there it was at the bottom of the container.

Another aspect of psychometry is flower readings. This most elegant form of psychometry is sometimes used in churches. I witnessed this when I visited Camp Chesterfield in Indiana. In fact, I received my first message at the camp during a flower séance. Selecting a yellow gladiola, the Rev. Glenda Freeman came to me and said, "I am holding a flower, but I am impressed to hold it like a pen. I feel you have something to do with writing?" She was, of course, correct.

In conclusion, the benefits from psychometry are many. They include locating lost object, finding jobs, finding better relationships, improving decision making, and contacting dead relatives, as well as viewing both the past and future. On the next page is the protocol for psychometry that is used at the New England School of Metaphysics.

Client _____ Date _____

Psychometry Session

1. Obtain a small object such as a watch or a ring from a friend, belonging to someone they know. They should know the history of the object, but the history is not revealed to you.

2. Hold the object in your hand and gain rapport. It is important to not worry about making a mistake at this point. Simply say what you are feeling. Is the person warm or cold, happy or sad, outgoing or shy? Do you feel male or female energy?

3. Now go beneath the surface. Try to find some simple details. Think about character and personality. What about health, both mental and psychological? Focus on past, present, and future one at a time.

4. Take moment to connect with your spirit guide. Is there any more information you can feel? If so, share it.

5. Now ask your friend what percentage you got right. Immediate feedback is important.

Notes

Suggested Reading

Ted Andrews, *How To Do Psychic Readings through Touch*

Joseph Rodes Buchanan, *Manual of Psychometry: The Dawn of a New Civilization*

W. E. Butler, *How to Read the Aura and Practice Psychometry, Telepathy, and Clairvoyance*

Suzy Chiazzari, *Flower Readings*

Sidney Flower, *A Course of Instruction in Development of Power Through Psychometry*

Sepharial, *Psychometry*

Kim Wright, mediumship student at New England School of Metaphysics, giving a psychometry reading to fellow student Driana Buonanducci.

Chapter Seven

Psychic Senses

It is not spirit that dwells in matter, but matter which clings
temporarily to spirit; and that the latter alone is an eternal,
imperishable abode for all things visible and invisible.

—Madame Helena Blavatsky

A PSYCHIC IS NOT A MEDIUM, but a medium is always psychic," the Rev. Gladys Custance explained to the Friday night group.

"Why?" we asked.

"That is because a psychic can use their intuition, but they do not connect with spirit. However, a medium connects with spirit through psychic senses and hence is always psychic."

Even today when I hear the term "psychic-medium," I think, "How redundant—a medium is always psychic."

However, opening the psychic senses is one of first stages of mediumship. During the three years I spent in Mrs. Custance's Friday night circle, my psychic senses of clairsentience and clairvoyance rapidly unfolded. Each of our physical senses has a "clair" or psychic counterpart. The term "clair" comes from the French for "clear." The four psychic senses are as fol-

lows:
- Clairsentience: psychic feeling
- Clairaudience: psychic hearing
- Clairvoyance: psychic seeing
- Clairgustience: psychic smelling or tasting

Most mediums tune into spirit by using these psychic senses. For instance, they might sense the presence of a grandmother in spirit, hear her name "Catherine," then see her face or even taste her apple pie. The message goes something like this: "I sense the spirit of a grandmother here—Catherine. She looks about seventy with gray hair in a neat bun and wire-rimmed glasses. She liked to bake—apple pies were her specialty."

Of course, it takes many years to reach this stage of psychic development. Often it begins with a feeling in the gut or clairsentience. Most everyone has had feelings that something is not right, accompanied by a queasy stomach or an uneasy feeling. Usually, the feeling is valid. Occasionally though, people have trouble trusting their intuition.

Also, it may be difficult to pinpoint the feeling. For example, one morning as Ron and I were driving to the grocery store, I suddenly felt depressed. Since I was basically in a happy mood, I attributed the sensation to my husband.

I said, "Please, Ron, stop thinking those distressing thoughts."

Ron responded with a quick but firm, "Elaine, I am not depressed." I believed him.

Still, the feeling persisted. I noted the time on the dashboard—10:15 a.m. Later in the day, our son Adam called with some upsetting news: "The bank turned us down for a mortgage, Mom."

"What time did that happen?" I inquired.

"Ten fifteen," he answered, in a soft voice. I certainly was clairsentient in the car that morning—but I was picking up Adam's depression, not Ron's.

The next psychic sense—clairaudience—can be disturbing if it is not properly understood. When people start hearing voices, they may feel like they are losing it, as auditory hallucinations can be a sign of mental illness. However, there is a big difference between a psychotic and a psychic. A psychic is in control of his or her clairaudience. If you do not wish to hear spirit, just send the thought and spirit will back away. The second difference is that the voices of a psychotic are negative and disturbing. This is because they are from negative spirits who require as much medical help as their host. Usually these people are tortured by negative spirits who give destructive commands. Often with antipsychotic medication, the auditory hallucinations are stilled. However, psychic development is not recommended for those diagnosed with mental illness. Neither is psychic unfoldment recommended for those who indulge in alcohol or drugs, as they too can be possessed.

Spirit is well aware of the need to develop psychic senses slowly in order not to disturb our psychological balance. That is why spiritual clairaudience is a gradual process of tuning into the voices of loved ones and guides.

Frequently it begins with a warmth or buzzing in one ear. Later, you may hear your name called from a distance. There is often the sound of voices coming through a tunnel, as spirit may form an astral tube to amplify their sound. When clairaudience is under more conscious control, the process is much like dialing a radio station to tune into spirit. I have sometimes observed public clairaudients lean toward spirit as they receive messages.

While many mediums utilize clairaudience, I find I am strongest in clairvoyance. I simply see the spirit in my inner eye with physical eyes closed. Sometimes spirit appears as a being of light when my eyes are open. Through clairvoyant investigation, I have learned much about life and death and have had the privilege of viewing the past and future for clients, as well as describing loved ones and guides.

The Hindus who locate the "eye of knowledge" in the middle of the forehead view opening the third eye of clairvoyance as a sacred task. They believe that opening the third eye will bring clairvoyance, precognition, and out-of body experiences. Taoists also advocate focusing attention on the point between the eyebrows with the eyes closed in various qigong postures. By doing so, students over time gain the ability to tune into the universe to reach advanced meditation levels.

My own clairvoyance began in my crib when I first spied my Hindu guide. When I was about five, he showed me how to open my third eye. Vividly, I remember the slender bare-chested guide with a white turban saying, "Cross your fingers and place them over the middle of your forehead. Now concentrate and push the energy out." Immediately a flood of bright lights came into my world. At the time I just accepted the lights. Later I realized that they were not from this world but from the other side.

It would be many years before I fully understood the significance of this practice. Basically, I was stimulating my third eye by lightly stimulating the optic nerves. Actually this practice has some physical basis. Western researchers, such Rick Strassman and Dr. Samuel Sagan, have situated the third eye with the pineal gland which is about the size of a pea. The pineal gland is located between the two hemispheres of the brain.

It is unusual to see spirit in full view, especially in the daylight. When you first experience clairvoyance, you will see tiny pinpoint lights— often white, blue, or purple about the size of a dime. This is more likely to occur in a dark room, as clairvoyants see better in darkness. With consistent practice, the full outline of spirit appears. Only experienced clairvoyants such as C. W. Leadbeater see the whole spirit all the time.

One excellent clairvoyant is the Rev. Rita Berkowitz. She combines clairvoyance with art to produce evidential portraits of deceased relatives and friends. When she visited the New England School of Metaphysics to give a workshop on "Spirit Art," I was thrilled to receive this wonderful likeness of my late grandfather, Harry Brickett (page 86).

Regardless of the degree of ability, everyone has the potential to open the third eye through meditation or a Spiritualist circle. Yogis use the candle meditation given at the end of this chapter to stimulate clairvoyance. Whatever method is chosen, they all work to raise the life force or kundalini energy which lies dormant at the base of the spine to the level of the third eye. If the kundalini energy reaches the throat level, clairaudience develops. At the heart level, inspiration, and on the stomach level, gut instinct.

Spiritualists use the weekly circle to develop psychic senses under the guidance of spirit. A second method is through the study of dreams— everyone has some psychic ability in the dream state. Pay particular attention to lucid dreams. The third method to open the third eye, universally accepted by East and West, is meditation.

In the circle, dreams and meditation, it takes time to open clairvoyance. In the East, the process of opening the third eye is sometimes hastened by procedures such as the one described in Lobsang Rampa's book *The Third Eye*. According to Rampa, a small hole was drilled into his forehead to stimulate clairvoyant sight: "A very hard, clean sliver of wood had been treated by fire and herbs and was slid down so that it just entered the hole in my head. I felt a stinging, tickling sensation apparently in the bridge of my nose. It subsided and I became aware of subtle scents which I could not identify. Suddenly there was a blinding flash. Lama Mingyar Dondup then told the initiate: "You are now one of us, Lobsang. For the rest of your life you will see people as they are and not as they pretend to be."[1]

Tibetan lamas also know how to astral project and travel the time lines. When Tibetan monks were cruelly persecuted by the Chinese in the late 1940s and 1950s, the monks showed remarkable self-control and mastery of the physical realm. One grim story told by Lama Yeshe and Lama Zope to students describes how many monks captured by the Red Chinese left their bodies at will: "Similarly, in the jails where so many of the monks and nuns were imprisoned and brutally tortured (a crime which is still being perpetuated to this day), they witnessed the remarkable sight of lamas quietly retiring to a corner of their cells, taking up meditation position, and, without further ado, simply leaving their bodies. They were neither sick nor dying, but were practicing powa, the transformation of consciousness to a different existence."[2]

Western adepts also abound in psychic powers. One of the most prolific Western clairvoyants was Charles Webster Leadbeater, author of *Clairvoyance* and *Occult Chemistry.* When Leadbeater, an Anglican priest, joined the Theosophical Society in 1883, he agreed to give up the church, become a vegetarian, and relocate to India with the founder, Madame Blavatsky. By 1895, he and Annie Besant, the society's second president, began to investigate the occult nature of chemistry. Leadbeater was able to peer into the structure of the atom before the microscope were invented. When science did invent microscopes powerful enough to peer into the atom, the structure was exactly as Leadbeater had depicted in *Occult Chemistry,* which was published in 1908.

Another theosophist who sought to understand the esoteric nature of man was A. E. Powell. He wrote a series of books on the etheric, astral, and causal bodies in the early 1900s. In *The Astral Body,* Powell describes its functions as follows: "To make sensation possible, to serve as a bridge between the mind and the physical body, and to act as an independently vehicle of consciousness."[2] It is in the dream state that the astral body functions independent of the physical. For spiritual aspirants, much can be gained from a study of dreams: "The dream life may be considerably modified as a direct result of mental growth. Every impulse sent by the mind to the physical brain has to pass through the astral body; as astral matter is far more responsive to thought vibrations than is physical matter, it follows that the effects produced on the astral body are correspondingly greater. Thus when a man has acquired mental control, i.e., has learned to dominate the brain, to concentrate, to think. As and when he likes, a corresponding change will take place in his astral life; and if he brings the memory of that life through into the physical brain, his dreams will become vivid, well-sustained, rational, and even instructive."[3]

Powell goes on to explain how, during sleep, the spiritual seeker may contact "Invisible Helpers". Powell also believes that "Mediums and psychics project their astral bodies unconsciously when they go into trance, but usually on coming out of trance there is no brain memory of the experience acquired."[4] He also asserts that "The astral body is also set free in many cases of disease."[5]

In the twentieth century, Sylvan Muldoon and Robert Monroe have written extensively on astral travel. In 1929, Muldoon coauthored a book, *The Projection of the Astral Body,* with Hereward Carrington. Convinced anyone could do astral projection, Muldoon and Carrington presented accounts of ordinary individuals who spontaneously left the body and safely returned. Muldoon, who had the had the ability to astral project at will, believed most people did so naturally in their sleep.

Years later approach, businessman Robert Monroe would come up with his own method for out-of-body experiences. His method of getting out of the body was to simply roll out. He believed most people could learn to leave their body if they knew how. Basically, there are three factors needed to successfully astral travel. First, the student needs to relax and enter a "borderline" state of sleep, through self-hypnosis. Affirmations such as "I will recall every detail in this state of relaxation" are recommended at this point. Once vibrations begin, Monroe advised this technique of separation: "Establish the vibration waves. As you continue breathing through your half-opened mouth, concentrate on the blackness in front of you with closed eyes. Look first into the blackness at a spot about a foot away from your forehead." Find a spot a foot from his forehead and move it out six feet. Monroe then advised: "Hold for a while until the point is firmly established. From there, turn the point 90 degrees upward on a line parallel to the body axis and reaching out above the head. Reach for the vibration at that spot."[7] Once the astral travel student is out of the body, the next step is to control the vibration and direct the trip. This, of course, comes with practice.

One famous participant in the Monroe Institute was remote viewer, Joseph McMoneagle. Remote viewing, by the way, is a form of controlled clairvoyance. On December 28, 1983, he was given these instructions by Robert Monroe: "Now you are at the library. Tell us something about the target in the envelope." The target was a slip of paper that said: "Who or what was Jesus and why was he here?"

This was McMoneagle's response to the query: "Joe: In the case of this manifestation, this man I am calling Christ. It was to show that there is no such thing as fear... other than self-imposed creation. But... he did all of this in a very mystical way, though it originally wasn't meant to be. I sense history played a hand in the over-mystification of the message."[8]

McMoneagle remote-viewed the future as well as the past. In his book *The Ultimate Time Machine,* he predicts a world that is downsizing with significant restrictions on its citizens: "By 2010-2012 most Western countries will be suffering economically." Among his more positive predictions are new forms of high speed electromagnetic monorails being used and more control over teenagers with anti-gang legislation (2015) tracking devices for teens (2020).[9]

Over the years as I have grown as a clairvoyant, I have received my share of prophecies. One of the most startling occurred a week before September 11, 2001, when a client, Cindy asked about a trip to New York City. Spirit advised her not to go.

"I see an airplane crashing into a window— it's not safe to go into New York," I added in trance.

Along with the gift of prophecy, I have also learned to respect the precious gift of life. Many times I will see a spirit child next to his or her mother who cannot be immediately placed. For example, a client of mine always had a spirit boy about age twelve close by. When I mentioned this, she was perplexed, so I asked her gently, "What happened about twelve years ago regarding a child?" She answered, "I had an abortion. My husband was shipping off for a six-month tour of duty and it just wasn't convenient to have a child at that time." While I do try to remain non-judgmental during session, I could not help but feel sad.

Based on clairvoyant observation, I agree with Tibetan Buddhists, who believe that life begins at conception and view abortion as an obstacle to spiritual progression. As I have grown as a clairvoyant over the years, I have also been touched by how much an interest spirit takes in our progress. For example, Ron and I went to New York City in 2007 to attend a Hoyt Robinette spirit card séance.

It turned out the hotel I booked was in a shady, inner-city location. I was a bit nervous, waiting for the bus to Manhattan. As I glanced over to my husband I saw the angel Gabriel standing about five feet from us. My heart just ached at the sight of an angel watching over us. The pure love and devotion of spirit never ceases to touch me.

More than anything, the devotion of loved ones and guides make the effort to communicate possible. However, it is important to remember that mediumship is a collaborative effort between spirit, medium, and sitter. Many times spirit is correct with the information but the individual is skeptical. Nothing is more deadly to a séance than a skeptic. This is especially true when on stage. In 1983, I was giving messages on the stage of a local college when I came to one student in the third row, a twenty-year- old, crew-cut wearing a blue shirt, named Jason, I had the following conversation:

Medium: "I feel you are going to have a career change quite soon. In fact I can see you taking an exam."

Jason: "No"

Medium: "Well I see you taking an exam- a civil service exam."

Jason: "No, that's not true."

Confused, I turned to spirit and said, what is the message, and clairaudiently heard- "He is going to get a job a the post office."

Medium: " I am sorry, I can't change the message. Spirit says you are going to get a job at the post office."

Jason's defiant manner was repleaced by a sheepish grin on his face, he took a piece of paper out of his pocket. " That's good news. I am taking post office exam this Saturday!"

Sometimes the sitter is a skeptic who just isn't going to admit anything—

unless pressed!

Other times a sitter may just be nervous. Once, I was doing private readings at a beauty salon in the back room. for a middle-age lady named Marcy.

Medium: "Joseph is here."

Marcy: "No, I don't know any Josephs."

When I turned to spirit for help, I heard Joseph on my right and my left, so I replied, " There are two Josephs here."

Marcy, "I am sorry, but I don't know any Joseph."

Sensing a father vibration, I said to Marcy, "Is your father in spirit?

Marcy: "Yes."

Medium: "What was his name?"

Marcy: "Joseph."

Then I sensed the two Josephs were related, so I asked "What was his father's name?"

Marcy laughed, "Joseph!"

While Marcy was too nervous to even remember her father and grandfather, others come to the office with one or two questions on their mind unaware that spirit is preparing them for possible futures. Jennifer, an attractive and intelligent blond, divorcee came to see me about once a year. Often she asked about a new love or job prospects, and, of course, her two sons. One of her sons, Peter, was a twenty-five year old who had had his problems with drugs and schizophrenia, but was doing better and living on his own. Since Jennifer had just inherited some money, she wanted to provide for him.

Jennifer: "Should I put some of my inheritance in a trust for Peter?"

Spirit: "Tell her no, she will outlive Peter."

Immediately, I sent the thought out to spirit, "I can't tell her that. Jennifer will be devastated."

Spirit: "Just give the message, we will answer a follow-up question if she has one."

Medium: "Spirit says, it is not necessary as you will outlive your son."

Jennifer then went on to another question. Sadly, Peter committed suicide within the year when schizophrenia returned after he had been in remission for some time.

Sometimes the sitter is the one who is mentally ill. If I know about it in advance, I send them to a psychologist. However, a regular client can develop mental illness, such as Nancy, a parapsychology student whose life was not going well. She had been seeing a therapist that I sent her to, but on occasion she asked for a reading. Since she was doing better, I agreed to see her. When the thirty-five-year-old secretary came into the office, I knew immediately she needed to return to her therapist. Why? Her aura was half purple (seeking help) and half black (possession). I did this brief session with Nancy:

Medium: "There is a priest in back of you who is trying to help you. He says you have been very depressed."

Nancy: "Who wouldn't be, with the government spies following me around all the time? They hired agents who look like normal people."

Medium: "No, that is your imagination. You need to talk this one over with your therapist."

When Nancy, tried to pay me, I refused, saying, "You need to call your therapist today—use the money for a session." Unfortunately, Nancy did not take my advice and was picked up by the police after she stopped her car in Hartford and accused some neighborhood teen-aged boys of being spies. Of course, when she called the police to arrest them, she was taken by the police to Hartford Hospital for psychiatric evaluation,

Maria was another disturbed client who sashayed in for a reading. The beautiful Hispanic mother of two was married to a hard-working husband, but was seeing a much younger man on the side.

Maria: "Is my boyfriend going to marry me?"

Medium: "I don't think so. I see him leaving the state."

Maria: "Yes, Barry is going out of state— just for a vacation—he needs some time to think. He is crazy about me."

Medium: "Going away by himself doesn't sound like someone in love."

At this point Maria's composure slipped. She stopped the session and demanded the tape be taken out of the tape recorder. She then proceeded to dismantle the tape furiously and threw the destroyed cassette into the wastebasket. Again, I refused a fee and urged her to see a counselor. Through a mutual friend, I heard Maria later had a nervous breakdown when Barry did not return to Connecticut.

While spirit was unable to reach Maria, other clients have benefited from spirit's guidance. One such case was a fifty-year old social worker who came regularly for sessions. When Rosemary sat down, I saw a gray spot in her etheric body right over her left breast. While it is illegal to give a medical diagnosis, there is nothing wrong in suggesting a client get a medical checkup, so I urged her see to a doctor immediately. She did. Diagnosis: breast cancer. Rosemary had a lumpectomy and is doing quite well ten years later. Naturally, I would like to help all my clients; however, some are more open to advice from spirit than others.

By the way, many woman receive the news they are pregnant from the spirit world. One client, Lucille, single and fancy-free came into to discuss her boyfriend, Harry. When I looked into her aura, I saw an etheric cord from her aura to a tiny spirit body.

"I see a baby-a lovely little girl coming into your life."

"No," Lucille corrected me (and spirit), "I just have the flu."

When she came for her annual reading the following year, Lucille brought baby Lily in to show me!

Of course, no medium is always right. However, with help from spirit and a cooperative client, a good medium is about eighty percent correct. Why? Free will. We can change some predictions by applying our free will. This is especially true in the case of accidents. Future mishaps can be sensed by psychics. For example, a lovely woman from Manhattan drove in for a session. I immediately sensed a pain in my right shoulder and back.

"No," Jody said, "my back and shoulder are fine."

The message made no sense at the time. However, two days later Jody called from the hospital to tell me her back and right shoulder were injured in a recent car accident. Apparently, the accident showed up in her aura ahead of schedule. If Jody had realized this, she might have averted the accident and the message happily would not have come true.

Another reason that a message may not be a hundred percent correct is that the timing may be off. An event predicted for one year may occur a year later. I found this to be true when the Rev. Gladys Custance saw me meeting someone in August 1971.

Reading April 1971

Messages given by Professor through the medium Gladys Custance:

Professor: "I see you meeting Mr. Right in August. He is just a few inches taller than you."

Elaine Marshall: "Well, I am not seeing anyone now. Am I going back with an old boyfriend?"

Professor: "No, you will meet someone new in August. He's seems very sincere and will want to get married quite soon."

August 1971 came and went with no new boyfriend. Confused and a bit lonely, I was puzzled by Professor's prediction. Mrs. Custance's guide was seldom wrong. As for Mrs. Custance, a trance medium, she had no conscious knowledge of her guide's messages, so the subject was never mentioned again. In August 1972, Professor's forecast came true when I met my future husband, Ronald Kuzmeskus, who is a few inches taller than I am. Happily, the Rev. Kenneth Custance and the Rev. Gladys Custance officiated at our wedding, November 18, 1972.

Author and husband Ronald Kuzmeskus with the Rev. Kenneth Custance
and the Rev. Gladys Custance on our wedding day, November 18, 1972.

End Notes

1. Lobsang Rampa, *The Third Eye*, Ballantine Books, New York, 1964.

2. Vickie Mackenzie, *Born in the West*, Marlowe & Company, New York, NY, 1996, page 7.

3. A. E. Powell, *The Astral Body*, The Theosophical Publishing House, Wheaton, IL, 1927, page 23.

4. A. E. Powell, *The Astral Body*, The Theosophical Publishing House, Wheaton, IL, 1927, page 95.

5. A. E. Powell, *The Astral Body*, The Theosophical Publishing House, Wheaton, IL, 1927, page 106.

6. A. E. Powell, *The Astral Body*, The Theosophical Publishing House, Wheaton, IL, 1927, page 106.

7. Robert Monroe, *Journeys Out of the Body*, page 213.

8. Robert Monroe, *Journeys Out of the Body*, page 213.

Grandparents Harry and Kathryn Brickett.

Portrait of Harry Brickett by psychic artist Rev. Rita Berkowitz.

Penny Hewitt, Assistant Director of the New England School
of Metaphysics, introducing students during Students' Night.

9. Joseph McMoneagle, *The Ultimate Time Machine,* Hampton Road Publishing Company, Charlottesville, VA, page 8.

10. Joseph McMoneagle, *The Ultimate Time Machine,* Part II, Hampton Road Publishing Company, Charlottesville, VA.

Candle Meditation

Meditation brings both inner peace and harmony. It also helps to build up the aura and add protection to your life force. Over a period of regular practice, meditation can help develop the gifts of telepathy, clairvoyance, and mediumship. The key to all meditation is regular practice.

One of the best yogi exercise is the candle meditation. Sit in a chair in a comfortable position with feet on the floor. Place a candle on a table opposite you at eye level, about an arm's length away. Gaze steadily at the candle for a minute. Then close your eyes and follow the after image in your mind's eye. Try to hold the image in your third eye as long as you can. If the image floats away from your gaze, concentrate on bringing it back and holding it steady. Allow your consciousness to remain steady, focusing on the image of the flame.

For maximum benefit, practice this exercise at the same time and place each day. Gradually lengthen your meditation time from five to twenty minutes, as you become more comfortable. Many students report telepathy, clairvoyance, and mediumship experiences after a period of about ninety days.

Target Technique for Two

Jane Roberts, who channeled Seth, used to put up a picture weekly in her office of an object, person, or scene for students use as a target. Try the same exercise with a friend. Have a friend put a picture up in a space in their home that you are familiar with. Alternately, an object may be placed for you to astral-view. In your sleep, give yourself the suggestion to visit and view the object. With practice, students begin to see the colors, shapes, or words that are in the picture.

Suggested Reading

Chaney, Earlyne, *Initiation in the Great Pyramid*

Chodron, Prema, *When Things Fall Apart*

Haith, Elisabeth, *Initiation*

Hall, Judy, *The Art of Psychic Protection*

Leadbeater, C. W., *Clairvoyance*

                Occult Chemistry

Mackenzie, Vickie, *Reborn in the West*

MeMonealge, Joseph, *Remote Viewing Handbook*

Powell, A. E., *The Astral Body*

              The Etheric Double

Reed, Henry, *Your Mind: Unlocking Your Hidden Powers*

Rampa, Lobsang, *The Third Eye*

            You Forever

Sagan, Dr. Samuel, *Entity Possession*

Spaulding, Baird T., *Life and Teachings of the Masters of the Far East*

Todeschi, Kevin, *Edgar Cayce on the Akashic Records*

Chapter Eight

Séance

The highest good is like water. Water gives life to the ten thousand things and does not strive. It flows in places men reject and so is like the Tao.   —Tao Te Ching

Once you have opened up the psychic senses, you can use clairsentience, clairaudience, clairvoyance, and clairgustience to identify spirit. This can be done in a private session or in a formal séance. Here are seven suggestions to prepare yourself for a séance:

One : Meditate for at least thirty minutes, preferably an hour, as close to the séance as possible. Spirit likes to fine tune your energy in the meditative state.

Two: Both medium and sitter should avoid alcoholic beverages and intoxicating drugs; they draw negative spirits.

Three: Begin with a prayer and have faith.

Four: Keep a respectful attitude toward spirit. Remember, like attracts like.

Five: As a medium, remember you are in control.

Six: Maintain a positive attitude and a sense of humor throughout the séance.

Seven: Speak directly to spirit.

It is also important to prepare the séance room. The Rev. Suzanne Greer uses a finished room in her basement which she keeps as dark as possible. In it are a cabinet, trumpets, and musical instruments for spirit to play. This is the ideal situation. However, some of us may need to use the dining room for a séance. This is fine as long as you can make the room dark and have sufficient seats for the sitters. Whatever room you use, make sure it is vac-uumed, dusted, and clear of clutter. Make sure that the room is as quiet as possible, with the telephone disconnected. Put a tape recorder with fresh batteries in the center of the table to record messages, and a glass of water should be placed in front of the medium and each of the sitters. The water will act as a conductor for psychic energy, as well as a thirst quencher. Fresh flowers are another nice touch. Also, take time to smudge the room with either sage or incense. I prefer Nag Champa or sandalwood incense. Then mentally call in your guides. Ask for the protection and assistance. Finally, I like to request an angel for each corner of the room and a spiritual gate-keeper at the door.

Set a time for your séance, say 8:00 p.m. If you are going to do forty-five minutes at spirit flame cards or an introductory talk, people can arrive at 7:00. Take a ten-minute break before the séance. Everyone should be seat-ed and in place at 8:00. Since Spirit is on time for appointments, we should be as well. I realized just how punctual spirit is when an out-of-town guest speaker arrived about ten minutes late. I noticed how the room filled up with her guides at the appointed time.

With a formal séance, certain rules need to be observed. The first rule is always to have an enthusiastic group. Spirit likes a light and positive atmos-phere. For this reason, warm up the audience with a short talk, or flame cards.

For newcomers, instruction is essential. I find my "three principles talk" works best. I interweave stories, facts and statistics to make the following three points:

One: We exist in a world beyond our five senses which a psychic can tune into through clairsentience, clairaudience, clairvoyance, and clairgustience.

Two: We continue to exist past the change called death-a fact scientifically proven by mediumship.

Three: The only way to cheat fate is to change our thinking. Thoughts are things. Positive thoughts lead to positive results, negative thoughts, to negative results.

Another way to warm up a group is the use of flame cards. People just love it! I have each sitter select a three by five white index card. Then I call on my guides and their guides to be present as they pass the card over a candle flame, being careful not to burn it. On page 129 is an example of a flame card. On one occasion, the Rev. Gail Hicks did a flame card for me with a diamond-shaped faceted jewel accompanied by the message "Jewel of the Nile" and than proceeded to give me message from my Egyptian guide.

After we take a short break, we assemble around the dining-room table for the formal séance. I have prepared the séance room beforehand by cleaning and clearing all negative energy. Usually I clear by smudging with incense, plus prayers of intent. I also like to have fresh flowers in the room, a glass of water in front of each sitter, and a tape recorder in the middle of the table.

The medium should make an effort to dress for the occasion. For an evening séance, a female medium should wear a long skirt, a gentleman a dark suit or sports coat. For a day ceremony, business attire is fine. The elegantly dressed medium sits at the head of the table and another medium who acts as a control or gatekeeper sits at the other end. At the New England School of Metaphysics, I usually sit at one end and our assistant director, Penny Hewitt, sits opposite, close to the door. It is her job as gatekeeper to keep order and make sure no one enters or leaves the room while the medium is in trance. To do so would be detrimental to the energy and ultimately to the séance. Also, no one is allowed to touch or disturb the medium who is in trance. To do so would be a shock to the medium's system.

Once we are all seated, we hold hands and say a prayer of intention. Some mediums prefer the group to continue to hold hands through the whole séance. Others, like myself, simply allow the group to place their hands in a comfortable position once contact is made. Then the group sings songs to raise the vibration. We like to sing classics such as "Jingle Bells," "I've Been Working on the Railroad," and "You Are My Sunshine."

Wait patiently for spirit to come through the medium. As Larry Dweller, author of *The Beginners Guide to Mediumship*, cautions, "Don't be impatient for contact. It will either flow or won't flow." Let the sitters know beforehand, spirit contact takes time. Many participants report that they feel a change of energy or a charged atmosphere at this point. Dweller points out: "Remember two very important things: the spirits of the departed are everywhere in the parallel dimensions (astral plane and higher planes).and the only reality spirits have in our own dimension is what we give them. By the intensity of our vibration level for reception, our intense faith, we draw them near to us."[1]

Contact can take a few minutes for loved ones to come through with messages. Sometimes questions are taken from the other side. For instance, a séance I gave in my office for students of the New England School of Metaphysics contained examples of spirit contact and advice on how to contact spirit. I was particularly pleased to hear from my mother, Dorothy Courtney, who had died on March 6, 2008.

Séances can also be done as Billet Séances. On page 101 is an example of a billet the sitter is asked to fill out. When they sign their name, spirit receives their question. The medium then says a prayer with the group, such as the Lord's Prayer, and then using psychometry holds each billet and gives his or her impressions.

By the way, no one does a better billet séance than the Rev. Hoyt Robinette from Camp Chesterfield in Indiana. On August 14, 2008, he conducted a billet séance in Suffield, Connecticut, for twenty-five people. He quickly gave me the names of my guides—Jack (Jack Kerouac) very close, Edwards (Harry Edwards), Bright Star (an American Indian guide), and the Rev. Kenneth Custance, who was not only my minister but my harp teacher. His message: "Get back on that harp."

Ron received beautiful messages as well from Ann (Aunt Ann), Tony (father, Anthony Kuzmeskus), Joe (Uncle Joe), and guides Ashtar (the Ashtar Command) and Chief Tonawanda (American Indian). His billet message: "Things are going to be good—real good in the cabinet. You are going to one country and many spots. Peru will be there too." Dr. Kenner (Hoyt's guide) said, "I have been asked to put Mary and Joseph on your card." When Ron received his spirit card, here was a picture of Mary and Joseph, which appears on page 138.

Another form of the séance is the public presentation. While a medium is able to set up the environment in the séance room for a public séance, he or she needs to be flexible with the rules. For example, at the Official Houdini Séance, at the Goodspeed Opera House, East Haddam, Connecticut, I had no say over who would attend, which meant the vibrations would be dicey.

In general, I am ambivalent about conducting public séances because I feel that they can be misused for publicity or sensationalism. There is no guarantee that spirit is willing or capable of making contact. This is often true when people first pass over—they simply do not have the energy to come through. As I tell my clients, I can't guarantee if a loved one will be present, but if they're in the room, I will bring them through.

In the case of Harry Houdini, his spirit had time to acclimate and would be able to come through if he wished to be present. However, I had another concern. It had been seventy-one years since Houdini's death. He might well have incarnated during this period or simply not wish to return. However, I did agree to conduct the Houdini séance on the strength of a message from the deceased medium Arthur Ford. He said simply, "Houdini has a message for you."

Tuesday (two days before the Halloween séance) I was in a panic. No further messages came through from either the Reverend Ford or Harry Houdini. Miffed, I sent the thought out, "I need to at least make contact with Houdini once before the séance." My guides quickly responded And a few minutes later the spirit of Harry Houdini appeared dressed to the nines in an elegant 1920s tuxedo.

On the day of the séance, I was excited and determined to do my best. I had arranged the séance to begin with a traditional Spiritualist message ceremony for the audience, which numbered about four hundred. The message service was perfect. Everyone recognized the spirits and agreed with the descriptions of deceased loved ones, as well as details regarding their personal lives. It was my finest message service. No wonder. I sensed plenty of help from spirit mediums on the other side, including the Rev. Arthur Ford, British medium Peggy Mason, and my teacher the Rev. Gladys Custance.

Then I had the light dimmed and a tape of "Inward Harmony" played so that people could meditate and reach their own loved ones. One student, Sheila, told me later, "My mother and husband came through as I meditated. It was so real." Spirit workers did a splendid job of bringing in loved ones and guides during the meditation, which lasted about five minutes.

However, once the formal stage séance began at midnight, the supercharged atmosphere was marred by dissenting thoughts. While assistant medium Barbara Dryden-Masse and myself believed in spirit communication, no one else seemed to believe it was possible for Houdini to contact us, including the master of ceremonies, Sidney Radner.

While I knew it was not going to be a perfect atmosphere, I wasn't prepared for all the doubt. Nothing is more deadly to a séance than doubt!

Once the preliminaries were over, I began the 1997 Official Houdini Séance by having all twelve participant hold hands and focus on Houdini. Then I did what I would normally do with a group of twelve. I went from person to person and identified the spirit present and shared brief messages. When I reached the actor who portrayed Harry Houdini, Timothy Gulan,

Houdini did come in. He encouraged the actor to continue acting. Houdini also told Gulan that he had been around the young man when he injured his shoulder and had decided to cancel that night's performance. Houdini, who by the way had been assisting him with the magic tricks from spirit, urged Gulan to go on, which he did. Gulan acknowledged this communication as valid. He had indeed injured his shoulder. Houdini, master showman, also had comments about the play, which he felt was too long. He urged writers to work on the humor in the script. The séance seemed to be going along well enough, so I allowed Barbara time to give some messages. As she paused to tune in, she was abruptly cut off by Sidney Radner. He then thrust an envelop in front of me and demanded to know the content. All I could feel was a letter with Houdini's signature. Spirit was not happy with this change in plans and backed away. Mentally, I asked my guides for help.

"Say nothing more," was the response from spirit. I fell back on remote viewing and traced the letter back to an oak frame in a glass display.

"No," barked Radner. He later confessed he knew nothing of where the owner of the letter kept it.

At the lackluster conclusion of the séance, Radner pronounced the séance a failure because the spirit of Houdini did not open the handcuffs placed in front me. Do I think Houdini came through? Yes, just for a few minutes for the actor who had the honor of portraying the great magician in the play, Timothy Gulan.

The format I put together is a sound one. By using a message service prior to the stage séance, I was able to warm up the audience, and the five-minute meditation added to the rapport. A medium needs to be in control of spirit. However, once doubt crept in on stage, spirit contact was limited. In the final analysis, those who truly did believe benefited from from the séance's messages and also received personal messages from their loved ones. For the unbelievers, it was just another show.

After the Houdini Séance experience, I would advise any medium to think carefully before agreeing to a public séance. Who will be included in the séance circle? What are their motives? Be prepared for less than ideal conditions. Finally, ask your guides for advice before accepting. If you are told by spirit to accept, have faith in spirit to pitch in as needed.

End Notes

1. Larry Dweller, *Beginner's Guide to Mediumship,* page 57

Suggested Reading

Berkowitz, Rita, and Deborah Romain, *The Complete Idiot's Guide to Communicating with Spirit*

Ford, Arthur, *Known But Unknown*

Ford, Arthur, *Life Beyond Death*

Northrop, Suzanne, *Séance: A Guide for the Living*

Billet Séance Exercise

Séances can also be done as Billet Séances. Here is an example of a billet the sitter is asked to fill out. When they sign their name, spirit receives their question. The medium then says a prayer with the group, such as the Lord's Prayer, and then using psychometry holds each billet and gives his or her impression.

Billet

Write the name of three people in the spirit world that you would like to contact and one question for spirit. Then sign the billet and date it.

_____

_____

_____

Question: _____

_____

Signature: _____

Date: _____

MEMBERS OF THE INNER CIRCLE

Sidney H. Radner . . . . .Séance Director

Thomas J. Boldt . . . . .Executive President, The Houdini
Historical Society

Dr. Morris Young . . . . .Magic Historian

Geno Munari . . . . .Owner of Houdini's in Las Vegas

John Gaughan . . . . .Illusion Department

Geno Gamache . . . . .Coyote Productions, Producer
Doumentary film: "Houdini"

Tony Wild .Co-Author of Houdini's Screenplay

Larry Weeks . . . . .Houdini Historian and Collector

Anna Crankshaw . . . . .Great-Granddaughter of the Psychic
Margery Crandon

Timothy Gulan . . . . .Harry Houdini in the Musical
Houdini

Lewis Cleale . . . . .Theo, Houdini's brother in the
Musical *Houdini*

Elaine Kuzmeskus . . . . .Spiritualist Medium

Barbara Dryden-Masse . . . . .Psychic

Facsimile of Houdini Seance Program

Chapter Nine

Trance

Under all circumstances, keep an even mind.

—Rev. Andrew Jackson Davis

S pirit has a way of gradually taking over the medium. For some mediums this can mean a light state of trance. For others, spirit can incorporate to achieve full trance. It is a fascinating process to allow spirit to take over completely. It all begins with deep breathing, Then there is a feeling of light-headedness, followed by a pull on the vocal chords as spirit enters. Sometimes I can hear a strange voice coming out of my mouth. Often I am in such a deep state I cannot remember what is being said and am completely surprised when I hear the recording later.

Many guides come in. Since I am a Spiritualist, I seem to attract the spirits of Spiritualist mediums such as Gladys Custance, Kenneth Custance, Arthur Ford, and Ivy, a deceased British medium. Ivy reminded students that the guides are not here for frivolous purposes but "come in to demonstrate to the world that those on the other side with greater knowledge, purer hearts, and finer attributes wish to assist when called upon."

It took many years to develop trance, as I did not start out as a trance medium. When I received my mediumship papers from the National Association of Spiritualist Churches in 1972, they read "Elaine Marshall, mental medium." I just chuckled. "I guess a lot of folks would consider a medium, mental."

All kidding aside, mediumship takes time and effort to develop. A medium in training does go through stages of development—one of which is opening the psychic senses. Mental mediumship develops with clairsentience, then progresses to clairaudience and clairvoyance. It can take many years of sitting in a circle to connect with the spirit world.

Only after I sat in the Rev. Gladys Custance's Friday circle for three years and served the First Spiritualist Church of Onset, Massachusetts, for two years was I allowed to take the written test for mediumship. This was followed by a test service in which my messages were validated by two other mediums in the audience.

After I completed my mediumship training in May of 1972, six months later, November 18, I married Ronald Kuzmeskus.

When we moved to Connecticut in 1973, I missed the Friday night circles, but I was able to continue to serve the First Spiritualist Church of Onset. I loved introducing the Custances to our children. First Adam, then Heather, and Kimberly, and finally Michael. As the children came along on the trips, we made it a point to make the visits a holiday. The children indulged in huge seafood platters served at Lindsay's Restaurant, played on the beach at Onset, and fished or roller-bladed along the canal.

As my mediumship progressed, I noticed that I was remembering less and less of the readings. It seemed as though I was drifting deeper and deeper into trance. For instance, I did a full hour reading after I had been to the dentist. My tooth felt fine during the session, but when I came out of trance, I realized that the Novocaine had indeed worn off and my mouth was smarting. Apparently, I was achieving quite a deep level of trance!

I had been practicing mediumship for about twenty-five years at the time. Now I felt I wanted to make a commitment to undertake trance training.

Trance is considered to be the strongest degree of control. While I had achieved a moderate level of trance, I knew I would need a teacher to achieve the full control known as "dead trance."

My venture into trance mediumship was also inspired by the great trance mediums I had met: Gladys Custance, Elwood Babbitt, and Gordon Michael Scallion. I saw firsthand how entering a trance state deepened the connection to spirit. For example, Mrs. Custance did readings, psychometry sessions, and classes all in trance, with Professor as a guide. We all looked forward to Professor's kindly instruction each Friday evening. I am only sorry that Mrs. Custance did not tape the sessions.

Elwood Babbitt, the second trance medium I met, did allow taping, and I have tapes of private sessions going back to 1981. This premiere channeler was born in Orange, Massachusetts, on November 26, 1922. From early childhood, he saw "spirit people." He recalled playing with friends and being very much upset when he walked right through one of them. When Elwood was sixteen, he had a very serious accident and doctors gave him a few hours to live. During the evening the spirit of his grandmother materialized before him. She told him that everything would be all right, that his eyes, ears, and throat, seriously damaged during the accident, would heal. He then saw a large ball of golden light over his head which went down through his whole body. Five days later, Elwood walked out of the hospital, to his doctors' amazement.

Two years later, in 1941, he joined the Marines. He happened to be stationed at Pearl Harbor on December 7, 1941, when the Japanese attacked the American fleet. He even saw the attack even before it started. However, he felt that the simple soldier he was would have no chance of convincing the authorities. He was an eyewitness to the destruction of the aircraft carrier *Arizona*. According to Babbitt, when the *Arizona* exploded, the gallant spirits of the 1,200 men aboard the doomed ship rose up in a white cloud.

What set Elwood Babbitt apart from other channelers were the evolved guides who spoke through Elwood. For example, he did a series of readings in which the Christ force manifested and the spirits of Jesus, his father Joseph, Luke the physician, the prophet Judy, and even Pontius Pilate talk about the life of Jesus. In 1981, this information became the book *Talks With Christ*, which was followed by *The God Within* in 1982. The books were coauthored by Dr. Charles Hapgood, who had been with Elwood since 1966 when he penned Babbitt's biography, *Voices of Spirit*.

One of Babbitt's most memorable channeling sessions took place in Boston in 1983. When the fifty participants formed a circle, you could hear a pin drop in the hotel ballroom as Elwood did the deep breathing required for trance. A full five minutes passed before we heard a voice with a distinct Indian accent identify himself as Mahatma Gandhi.

When Gandhi finished his discourse and allowed questions, we were all so stunned no one could speak. Finally, concerned we were losing momentum, I asked, "What can we do for world peace?" I have long forgotten the response but I will never forget the high vibration of energy present that February afternoon or the love that emanated from the spirit of Mahatma Gandhi as he spoke through Elwood Babbitt.

While Mahatma Gandhi's focus was on world peace, Dr. Fisher gave personal advice. I had private readings with Elwood every year from 1980 to 1999. Babbitt possessed a remarkable gift for channeling akin to that of Edgar Cayce. Like Cayce he also lived modestly in relative obscurity in rural western Massachusetts. Babbitt began each session by deep breathing for a few minutes, followed by the steady breathing of a deep sleep. Then with some effort, his facial expression would change as his control, Dr. Fisher, entered the body. Finally his cultured voice would announce: "Dr. Fisher here assuming control of the body."

There was a real incongruity between Elwood Babbitt, the ex-Marine who didn't even bother to finish high school, and the erudite Dr. Fisher, who was very much a gentleman in voice and mannerism. More than once, I made the mistake of addressing the entranced Elwood Babbitt as "Elwood" and received the reprimand, "This is Dr. Fisher speaking." Here is an except from a 1983 reading I received from Elwood Babbitt at his home in Orange Massachusetts:

> Dr Fisher assuming control of the body and observing new forces of energy moving into your spiritual self show you approach the zenith on the wheel of life. You shall have greater opportunities in teaching and service to others and to the intuitive voice and you shall obtain more self-realization in response to the forces around you at the present time.
>
> I have been in contact with the master forces that relate to your specific energies with your frequency or force and it is their request you practice GOD I AM DIVINE MIND. It will bring reactions of your spiritual self in a deeper way.

Ron and I were going through a lot of turmoil at the time, so I often said the affirmation, "God I am Divine mind," on my lunch hour! Dr. Fisher also told me that "two more souls await birth," which turned out to be true: we had a daughter, Kimberly, in 1984 and a son, Michael, in 1986.

Much of Elwood Babbitt's work also centered on upcoming earth changes, which mirror those predictions of Edgar Cayce. Once when asked about earth changes, Dr. Fisher emphatically told me that more than half of the world's population would perish in the coming Earth changes. He even moved to Maine at one point to prepare for the changes.

In the early '90s, I met another channeler who also predicted great physical changes for the United States—Gordon Michael Scallion. His predictions were also similar to those of Elwood Babbitt and Edgar Cayce. Scallion, a futurist, has made earth changes his focus, publishing a journal, *Earth Change Report*. Scallion's paranormal abilities developed quite suddenly. Like Cayce, he found himself unable to speak when he was giving a business presentation. During his brief hospitalization, Scallion was contacted by guides. Over the years, his fine-tune trance readings led to publication of a book, *Notes from the Cosmos,* along with the *Earth Change Report.*

Scallion's predictions for the future include severe earth changes in California and economic decline from 1998 to 2012, followed by a new spiritual awareness: "Wars are replaced by a spirit of cooperation. Food is shared globally through a system of food banks. Life in the new millennium is based on unity and respect for all life. If you were to ask various national leaders in the next millennium, 'What do you consider your country's most valuable treasure?' most would respond emphatically, "Our children!' "[1]

While Scallion and Babbit were excellent trance mediums, they were simply too busy to teach. Finding the right trance instructor was not going to be easy—very few mediums are qualified. I began my training for trance by signing up for a weekend workshop with Dr. Lauren Thibideau. Her two-day trance workshop was excellent. By the end of the seminar my friends and I were channeling. Ceil channeled an Egyptian princess. Another friend, Nancy channeled the angel Ariel, and I channeled the angel Azul. It was great fun, but I felt I needed much more training, so I asked Lauren, "Where is the best place to study trance?" Her reply: "The Arthur Findlay College, outside of London."

In June of 2003, Ron and I, along with friends Stanley and Mary Ellen, made the journey to England. When we arrived at the Arthur Findlay College, we were impressed by the beautiful surroundings. The college sits on acres of manicured lawn with its gardens in full bloom. Inside, the stately brick building is furnished with oil paintings of British aristocrats, oriental rugs, and priceless antiques.

The college was once the home of Scottish stockbroker and Spiritualist Arthur Findlay, who donated it to the Spiritualist Union. When I registered at the college, I couldn't help but notice Mr. Findlay's portrait facing me. His sharp stockbroker's eyes seemed to be checking out each person as they entered the college. His spirit is very much present—along with many other spirits. The very first night, I awoke to see men dressed in medieval armor parading through the room, followed by nuns in ancient garb. Apparently the site of the college goes back to Saxon times.

Once settled, I met our teacher Muriel Tennant, a veteran medium. She was fashionably dressed as one would expect from the former owner of a dress shop—which, by the way, turned out to be haunted. This experience led her to Spiritualism in the 1960s. This elegant medium led the class of twelve in trance exercises three times a day. During our first session, I sent out Reiki symbols to the group. Muriel was fit to be tied.

"Elaine," she said, "what are all those squiggly lines around you?" When I told her Reiki symbols, she implored, "Please do not send any symbols out. Allow spirit to contact you."

Ron and Stanley were in the same class with another American, a slender blonde medium from California. Their instructor, Maureen Murnan, was taken aback when the Californian announced she channeled Elvis Presley.

Once Maureen even asked this student to leave the group temporarily—not for channeling Elvis but for being depressed. Apparently, Maureen and Muriel both ran a tight ship—no negative thoughts or "squiggly lines" allowed!

On the second day, I took Muriel's advice and relaxed enough to let spirit do the work. Soon the group began to bond as we took turns going into trance. While four members went into trance for about twenty minutes to a half hour, the other eight members and our leader would observe the spirits and energy around the sitters. It was just fascinating, so many spirits were present.

On the second day, we also chose partners. The group had several from England, one medium from Australia, and another from Sweden—the rest from the United States and Canada. I chose Marcia, an Australian medium with a bright and very large yellow aura. I knew that she was one of most advanced channelers. It turned out we had a lot in common. Both of us had degrees in the medical field and were teaching classes in mediumship. Muriel was also impressed with Marcia and chose her to demonstrate channeling on guest night.

While some students like Marcia were advanced, others needed instruction. How did our group develop trance? It really was a gradual process of letting go. After six days of practice, I was really ready to let go and let spirit take over. My anxiety seemed to be holding me back. However, on the last day, I decided to take a walk with Marcia to get some money for our trip home. We both shared stories of visiting Sai Baba in India—another commonality.

The relaxing walk seemed to do the trick. When I returned for the last session, I just sank into trance, and a distinguished silver-haired gentleman and a grandmotherly woman were seen behind me. Eventually the woman overshadowed me and I channeled my beloved teacher Gladys Custance, with Kenneth Custance assisting.

Two years later, I took a group of advanced students to Camp Chesterfield for additional training. The students—Mary, Kim, Becky, and Nancy—joined Ron and me. We all very much enjoyed the trance classes with trance mediums Patricia Kennedy and Suzanne Greer. We had several sessions in Kennedy's home, which had once belong to the famed medium Austin Wallace. Her classes were similar to those at Arthur Findlay. Five of us observed while one student went into trance. The Reverend Kennedy had the student breath slowly, until Pat could see spirit around the student. At that point, she spoke directly to the entity: "Hello, friend. Can you tell us who you are?" It wasn't long before we heard answers such as "I come in peace," or, in my case, "Gladys."

The Rev. Suzanne Greer was also an expert teacher. She gave "Introduction to the Séance Room" classes. Her initial advice: "A séance is a team effort between sitter, spirit, and the medium." She emphasized that the medium needs to be well rested and needs to meditate before trance. As for the guides, "They need to be strong as well as the medium for transmission to take place."

"A strong medium," she stressed several times, "is in control of spirit." To emphasize her point she told us this story: One summer evening, the Rev. Bill English, the great trumpet medium, had just closed the door to his séance room when a visitor rang his bell. He hastily opened the door, and an excited lady asked to be included in his trumpet séance, stating emphatically, "My guides told me to attend." Without missing a beat, English replied, "Well, your guides didn't tell me," and firmly closed the door.

End Notes

1. Gordon Michael Scallion, *Notes From the Cosmos,* Matrix Institute, West Chesterfield, NH, 1997, page 289

Suggested Reading

Elwood Babbitt, *Perfect Health*
       Talks With Christ
       The Vishnu Testament
Peggy Barns, *Lo I Am With You Always*
Madame Blavatsky, *The Secret Doctrine*
Arthur Hasting, *On the Tongues of Angels*
Charles Hapgood, *Voices in Spirit*
N. Riley Heagerty, *The French Connection*
Sidney Kirkpatrick, *Edgar Cayce: An American Prophet*
Jon Klimo, *Channeling*
Gordon Michael Scallion, *Notes From the Cosmos*
Jess Stearn, *The Sleeping Prophet*
N. Alexander Wheeler, *The Prophetic Revelation of Paul Solomon*
Christine Wicker, *Lily Dale*
A Course in Miracles

Exercise:
Journey to the Akashic Library

One way to deepen trance is through guided imagery. Before you do this exercise, decide on a question or information you would like to receive from your book of life known as the akashic records. Lie or sit in a comfortable position and have a friend read the following hypnosis exercise:

Close your eyes. Take three deep breaths. We all have a book of life on the other side where your akashic records are kept by the masters. Here, you can look up any question and receive information. Your personal book of life is kept in a library on the other side staffed with religious people such as monks and nuns. It is your privilege to visit this library on the other side.

As you prepare for your journey, ask your guides to be with you.

Pause.

Take three deep breath. Breath in peace. Breath out stress. Surround yourself with the white light of protection. Imagine you are looking at a pool of aqua water with white lotus blossoms gently skimming the surface. Relax your eye muscles as you gaze at this beautiful scene.

Allow this feeling of relaxation to go into your forehead, erasing any stress—into your cheeks, ears mouth, throat—your entire face. You may wish to part your lips a bit just to relax your jaw.

Pause.

Now this feeling of relaxation is traveling down your neck into your shoulders, releasing all stress. Feel the relaxation travel down your spine.

Your spine is a flexible as a piece of spaghetti—every vertebra in place.

Next center the relaxation on your right shoulder and feel it travel down your right shoulder to your right elbow to your right wrist to your right fingertips Your whole right arm from the shoulder to fingertips is completely relaxed.

Pause.

Next center the relaxation on your left shoulder and feel it travel down your left shoulder to your left elbow to your left wrist to your left fingertips. Your whole left arm from the shoulder to fingertips is completely relaxed.

Allow the relaxation to enter your chest. Feel your breathing become more rhythmic. It is so easy to breathe in and out.

In and out.

Your heart is beating rhythmically. Soft, gentle beats.

Pause.

Next center the relaxation on your left hip and feel it travel down your left leg to your left thigh and your left ankle to your left foot. Your whole left leg from hip socket to the sole of your foot is completely relaxed.

Your whole body is completely at peace, totally relaxed. Your whole body is completely at peace, totally relaxed.

Pause.

Breathe deeply in through the nose and out through the mouth. Focus your attention on your third eye. Allow the area in the midst of your forehead to soften. Feel the energy expand as you focus on the third eye. Feel a bright light around your third eye—penetrating and opening it even wider. Feel a comforting, warm pulsation. Allow the light to open your inner vision completely. Focus this radiant light outward.

Pause.

See yourself in front of a spiral staircase. On the count of seven you will walk down each of the seven stairs. When I say "seven," but not before, you will be in an old library where your book of life is kept. Take your time, put your hand on the railing, and feel yourself going down seven stairs.

Elwood Babbitt, trance channeler.

One.

Two.

Three.

Four.

Five. Almost there.

Six.

And seven. You are now in the library. As you look around you can see a monk who is filled with compassion and wisdom. The library is quiet, a holy place of peace and calm. The monk goes to the book shelf and selects your book of life and places it on a table before you. You feel excited and happy. These are the akashic records, where the wisdom of all your lives is kept. In a moment as I say the number three you will open the book and find the answer to your question. Ask your question now. Put your hands on the book.

One.

Two.

Three.

Open to the page which has the answer to your question. As you open the book, you are astounded by the wisdom. Take a moment. You may see or sense the answer. Enjoy the book. I will give you three minutes. While you read the passages you will receive guidance.

Pause.

I will give you a few moments to gather more information.

Play soft music for three minutes.

Pause.

Very good.

You will remember all the details. Now you are about to return. Thank the monk. And start walking back up the stairs.

One. You are ready to return.

Two. You feel rested.

Three. You feel wonderful in every way.

Four. You have peace of mind.

Five. You are waking up.

Six. You are ready to come back.

Seven. Eyes wide awake.

Andrew Jackson Davis, trance medium.

Chapter Ten
Physical Phenomena

Another important aspect of mediumship is physical phenomena, which frequently begin with lights, breezes, and raps that every one in the séance room can witness. Most mediums begin with table tipping, electronic voice phenomena, or psychic photography, which do not require trance training. More advanced phases of physical mediumship include trumpet mediumship, direct voice, and materialization, which is done in deep or "dead" trance. While few mediums have the physical chemistry needed for trumpet mediumship or materialization, those who possess this ability sit in meditation for many years. As physical medium Hoyt Robinette explained: "I sat in meditation an hour a day for each of my gifts." His remarkable gifts, which include trumpet mediumship, spirit pictures on silk, and precipitated spirit cards, took seventeen years to develop.

My first experience of physical phenomena was in Gladys Custance's Friday night class. It was not unusual to see colored lights in the room and occasionally smell lilacs, roses, or tobacco. When these things occurred, everyone in the room experienced them. Sometimes we even heard raps.

By the way, I was quite startled the first time I heard spirit raps. The raps occurred in the parish house where I spent the summer of 1971. The Rev. Laurie Kirkpatrick and I were having a cup of tea. While we were quietly sipping our orange pekoe, loud raps came out of the china cabinet next to the dining room table. The raps, which literally shook the dishes in the cabinet, were quite loud. They were like nothing I had ever heard, as the sound seem to come from inside the mahogany cabinet as if someone were banging from inside. Laurie just laughed when she saw my startled face.

"Don't be alarmed," she said. "That's just my husband saying 'hello' from the other side. When he was alive, he was a proper Methodist minister who did not share my belief in psychic phenomena. Apparently he does now." Three more loud raps were heard as if in agreement to Laurie's last statement.

When Professor, Gladys Custance's guide, told me early in my training, I had the chemistry to be a physical medium, I had no desire to be one. To be honest, I found mental mediumship challenging enough. Later, the demands of raising four children, mediumship and teaching left little time for additional study. However, as the New Millennium approached, I had the time to take classes in trance, table tipping, electronic voice phenomena, and spirit flame cards.

When the College for Spiritual Knowledge hosted a seminar with the Rev. Lynn Kent and her husband the Rev. Brian Kent, I was eager to attend. Seven of us—Ron, five students, and I—took the trip to New London, Connecticut, to learn table tipping. Lynn Kent did a lecture on selecting the right table. She suggested a small lightweight table to begin. After picking the right table, it is important to cleanse it and dedicate the table to spirit.

Then the students sat around small, round tables in groups of three or four. We concentrated on spirit with meditation and then started to sing lively songs such as "I've Been working on the Railroad." At first my fingers felt sticky if they were melding into the table. Then with Lynn's assistance, the table began to move. At first, just a little bit. Then it was really moving back and forth, so we decided to establish a code for "yes," moving to the back of the room, and "no," moving to the front of the room. I asked the first question: "Is my grandfather here?" to which we got a "Yes." It was all great fun.

Later, we tried table tipping in class and actually got the three-legged table onto one leg. At one point the table walked out the living room, around the corner, and down the hall to my office. It seemed to have a mind of its own. Some students have even gotten the table to levitate off the ground a few inches.

While table tipping can be evidential, so can slate writing. When I visited the Lily Dale Museum, I was impressed by a slate that bore the handwriting and signature of Abraham Lincoln. According to curator Ron Nagy, author of *Slate Writing: Invisible Intelligence,* Abraham Lincoln signed several slates created by Lily Dale medium P. L. O. A. Keeler: "Many times Abraham Lincoln indicated his presence by signing his name. Many claim Lincoln was a Spiritualist or at least believed in its powers and has sent messages through the mediumship of Mr. Keeler."[1]

Abraham Lincoln also came through the art of the Campbell Brothers. In the Maplewood Hotel at Lily Dale Assembly there is portrait of Abraham Lincoln that was precipitated by the Campbell Brothers. According to curator, Ron Nagy, "No one knows exactly how, or under what circumstances, precipitated spirit paintings started, but as in most instances the first phenomena occurred with the mediums unaware of what was happening or why. The first recorded demonstration of precipitated spirit painting was in the year 1894 by the Bangs Sisters."[2]

Nothing is more convincing to the skeptic than orbs, outlines, and even faces of spirits. Some, like Boston engraver William H. Mumler (1832–1884) were able to capture the images of the deceased on film. Noted Victorian Spiritualist Emma Britten Hardinge visited Mummler's Boston studio at 285 Washington Street. When Mrs. Britten, a famous actress who became a medium, looked at her photograph, she was pleased to see the image of Beethoven standing behind her with his spirit arm protectively draped over her shoulder.

Mummler's most noted sitter was Mary Todd Lincoln, who used the alias of Mrs. Tyndall. Apparently, both President and Mrs. Lincoln were very

Orbs manifest during a ceremonial dance of native Brazilian Indians.
Photographer: Mary Arendt

interested in parapsychology and even had séances in the White House. It seems that after their son Willie's tragic death in the White House, Mrs. Lincoln turned to the medium Nettie Colburn for consultation. It was only natural that she would also seek to communicate with her deceased husband through Mummler. She was not disappointed. When her photographic plate was develop, Mrs. Lincoln was greeted by the shadowy figure of her late husband, President Lincoln, standing behind her.

Psychic photographs can take many forms. Sometimes spirit is captured on film in orbs which do not show up until the film is developed. This was the case when one of my students, Mary Arendt, joined Ron and me on a visit to John of God in 2007.

Mary, a second-grade teacher, was charmed by South American Indian children. When they invited her to attend one of their ceremonies, she agreed to come back that evening. When we returned from Brazil, I received an excited call from Mary: "Elaine, you won't believe what is on the orbs in the photo of Native Americans doing their ceremonial dance. These pictures all have orbs in them."

The pictures clearly document a few orbs (spirit) entering as the ceremony began, then more as it progressed, and finally an abundance of orbs at the height of the ceremony. In the left-hand corner of the third picture is an orb that resembles Our Lady of Guadalupe.

After taking picture of orbs, mists, and outlines of spirit, the next step is to take pictures in which spirit faces appear. An example of this occurred during a visit to Danbury in October of 2008. I was there to investigate the a ghost that rang the elevator around 9:00 p.m. each night. As I was waiting for the bell to ring (which it never did), I took a few random shots and was quite surprised to find one filled with the faces of spirit.

If you wish to capture faces, orbs, or outlines of spirit on film, here are some suggestions: First it is important to gain rapport with spirit. Then you can take a picture with a conventional camera or a digital one. It is not necessary to actually see the spirits. If they are there, they will show up on the developed film.

Another method of spirit photography is done on silk squares. I saw this firsthand when I attended a séance in Maryland conducted by the Rev. Hoyt Robinette. About twenty-five of us gathered in for a spirit on silk session with the Rev. Hoyt Robinette. He started by explaining how spirit would impress photographs of our loved ones on eight-inch white silk squares. Next he gave each of the participants an eight-inch square of silk.

Then the lights were turned out and the Reverend Robinette led the group in the Lord's Prayer. Almost immediately, he went into the deep state known as dead trance and his guide Dr. Kenner took over, giving us messages, as other spirits imprinted the images on the silk squares.

Finally, we were instructed to roll up the silks and the construction paper beneath them and keep them away from the light for twenty-four hours lest the images not develop completely. When I opened my silk the next day, I was happy to see a picture of my Aunt Ruth, who had passed to spirit in

1953.

Whatever method you use, psychic photography is not an exact science; it takes time to develop. Most psychic photographers agree that spirits will allow us to take their picture at the right time. Sometimes the spirits are shy, other times they will come in abundance. When you arrive at location, take a half hour or so to gain rapport. Walk around, see what energy you pick up. Note any changes in temperature, sparkly lights, or even fragrances. When ghost hunting I have found taking an EMF meter helpful.

Once a hot spot has been found, then take a photograph using a digital camera. These images are most common:

Orbs—The most common image in psychic photographs. They are round spheres that may be transparent; however, occasionally a face may appear in the middle of an orb.

Ghost lights—An illuminated orb or light. Sometimes it will have a distinct color.

Ectoplasm—Ectoplasm, which may appear as a fog or mist in a photograph, often in strategic areas. Faces or figures will sometimes form out of the substance.

If you wish, use an EMF meter to pinpoint a psychic area. Once a hot spot has been located, it is important to take a photograph immediately. For example, during séances, when orbs, mists, and even the full outline or body of a spirit appear, position a photographer opposite the medium to capture the phenomenon. Do not take a photograph while the medium is in trance, as the flash can jar both spirit and the medium. Sometimes a picture can be obtained if you ask permission beforehand. If possible use an infrared camera or turn off the flash on a regular camera so as not to disturb the medium. Be patient. Remember also to be clear in your intention and ask spirit permission before you enter their realm. Don't forget to surround yourself with white light and a prayer for protection such as: "We call on that which is for the highest good of each and ask that the loved ones, guides, and angels be present."

Next, place a glass of water beside each sitter, or if you prefer under each seat. Water is used as a conductor for ectoplasm. A glass is better than a paper cup because it seems to hold a charge of energy better. Be patient and wait for the medium or spirit guide to signal permission to take a picture. Sometimes the guide will point to places to photograph during the séance.

Any camera will do. Some experts prefer a digital one because it eliminates any criticism about flaws in the film. Whatever method you choose, don't expect results right away. If the conditions are right, orbs, lights, and ectoplasm can crop up in photos, but it may take several shots. Remember to examine your photos carefully, as orbs vary from a few inches to several feet in diameter. With practice, faces may appear in the center of the orbs.

Not only can the image of spirits be captured, so can the voice of spirits. Leslie Flint who was famous for this ability to manifest the voice of spirit, called himself "the most tested medium in England." He brought through this message from Mahatma Gandhi:

> The first lesson one must learn is to forget oneself, to give out in love all that is possible from within yourself, and it shall be returned to you. These things that Christ spoke about, and all the great teachers, all the great philosophers down through the ages, was that man should forget himself so that in return he might find himself.

If you would like to hear spirit voice, it is available at *www.LeslieFlint. com/recordingsmickey.html*.

In recent years, four friends, Robin and Sandy Foy and Diane and Alan Bennett, got together in Scole, England, to try their hand at Electronic Voice Phenomena. They contacted a guide named Manu and their efforts were richly rewarded with an EVP recording that included an audible performance of Rachmaninoff's Second Piano Concerto.

I first became interested in EVP when I was doing research for my book, *Séance 101*. I took a three-day workshop at Omega Holistic Institute in Rhinebeck, New York. The instructors, Tom and Lisa Butler, were the directors of the American Association for Electronic Voice Phenomena. They talked about using prayer and asking for protection before turning our tape recorders on. They also stressed the importance of talking to spirit. When I placed my tape recorder in the center of the circle, I asked, "Spirit, if you are here, please give me a message." Then I waited about two minutes for a response.

I was rewarded with two evidential EVPs: one from my husband's deceased father and the other from noted Connecticut medium Carl Hewitt, who had died that February. When I played the tape back for the group, we all heard "Protect…Anthony." I felt intuitively that Anthony was protecting our teen-aged son Michael. The next day, I tried the EVP experiment again and received a voice in the distinctive Southern drawl of the late Rev. Carl Hewitt speaking his name: "Carl."

With some patience and practice, most researchers can master the art of recording EVPs. First, you need a tape recorder, either a standard cassette recorder or a digital one. Many prefer the digital as it can be linked directly to the computer to amplify sound. Next, some form of white noise is needed for the spirit to create sounds. Use the sound of a hair dryer or even running water.

Now you are ready to select a location. Try a place where there has been some psychic activity such as an old abandoned building, a historic site, or even a cemetery. As you enter the site protect yourself by imagining a shield of white light around you and say a prayer. As always, take a moment to ask permission from spirit to record their voices.

Don't be afraid to question spirit. That is how the voice of Carl Hewitt came through. In the privacy of my room at Omega, I just sent the thought out: "Should I pursue EVP?" Within seconds, Carl answered in his familiar voice, "Keep going. You are close to a breakthrough."

Once you successfully record an EVP, it is helpful to use an voice amplifier, which can be purchased for less than fifty dollars at your local computer store. It is also helpful to use a device to graph the EVP, such as the Audition or Audacity sound editor, which amplify, filter, and even reverse a sound file.

According to Tom Butler, "You can either make the recording on a tape recorder and then play the tape into the computer for review, editing, and storage, or attach a microphone directly to the computer and use the sound editor as a tape recorder."

When transferring into a computer, make sure the computer is set for "Line In" recording in "Sound and Multimedia" in the Control Panel of your personal computer. If you must take sound from the earphone jack of your recorder, consider purchasing an attenuating cord to match the difference in resistance between the two jacks. Radio Shack can help.[3]

In addition to EVP, spirit may chose to manifest through levitation. One of the most amazing of the levitation mediums during the twentieth century was Jack Webber. During his brief career in the 1930s and '40s, Webber demonstrated his ability to materialize apports, levitate heavy tables, materialize ectoplasm, and manifest direct voice, table levitation, and ectoplasm. In his biography of Webber, Harry Edwards describes Webber's voices emanating from the trumpet.

> Clearly, too, without such force, Paddy (a boy control) is often heard, as is also the rich contralto voice of a lady, and other spirit singers. A phenomenon (impossible for human agency to reproduce) is the singing of Reuben and Paddy at the sane time through the same trumpet. The trumpet is generally well away from the medium, six to eight feet high, and a similar distance in front of the medium. It s interesting to remember that the diameter of the trumpet's mouth is half an inch, and after use this end becomes battered and beat so the orifice is partially closed. Under such

conditions, no human mouth could possibly use such a mouthpiece and produce the perfectly formed words of a hymn, slow, deliberate, and perfectly enunciated.[4]

In addition to the levitation of the trumpet, rolls of ectoplasm appeared. Webber while in trance was able to levitate tables weighting forty-five pounds into midair, all captured on infrared film. On occasion the medium's jacket was turned inside out by playful spirits while he was in trance. Unfortunately Webber's mediumship was short-lived, as he passed over to the spirit side of life at age thirty-three, just as his mediumship was becoming public.

I have seen my share of trumpet mediums at Camp Chesterfield and in the Boston area. In all, I have attended six to date: two with the Rev. Louise Irvine at Camp Chesterfield in which an ascended master came through two huge trumpets in pitch darkness, and one with the Rev. Suzanne Greer in which the trumpet actually touched each of us on the toes and we all received a personal message from the spirit.

The three most evidential trumpet séances were with the Rev. Hoyt Robinette. During the first one, the spirit of Harry Edwards came though and spoke to me about medical clairvoyance, the question I had decided to ask before the séance. We all received apports as well; mine is a gold cross with the praying hands on it. Others received stones and semi-precious jewels. At a second trumpet séance with the Rev. Hoyt Robinette, I was thrilled to hear the voice of the ascended master El Moyra, who came in to encourage further trance mediumship.

In addition to trumpet séance, the Reverend Hoyt does precipitated spirit cards in which faces of loved one, spirit guides, and even angels manifest on the three-by-five-inch index cards. In March 2009, one of our new students, Sylvia, invited her mother, a strict Catholic, to a spirit card séance, Her elderly mother worried that it might not be the right thing to do, so she prayed to Mother Mary to guide her. When she received her card, there was a picture of Mother Mary exactly like the one on her prayer card on her table at home. Mary also appeared on my husband Ron's spirit card. He was told by spirit that he would receive a picture of Mary and Joseph in their middle years.

End Notes

1. Ron Nagy, *Slate Writing: Invisible Intelligence*, 2008, Galde Press, Lakeville, MN, page 129.
2. http://www.ronnagy.net/
3. http://www.aaevp.com
4. Harry Edwards, *The Mediumship of Jack Weber*, Anchor Press Ltd, 1974, pages 84 and 85

Suggested Reading

Brealey, Gena and Kay Hunter, *The Two Worlds of Helen Duncan*

De Salvo, John, *Andrew Jackson Davis*

Foy, Robin, *In Pursuit of Physical Mediumship*

Jolly, Martyn, *Faces of the Living Dead*

Hallowell, Katie, *Experiences of Trance, Physical Mediumship, and Physical Phenomena in the Stewart Alexander Circle, Volumes I and II*

Kuzmeskus, Elaine, *Séance 101: Physical Mediumship, Table Tipping and Other Important Physical Phenomena*

O'Hara, Gerald, *Dead Men's Embers*

Nagy, Ron, *Precipitated Spirit Paintings*
        Slate Writing: Invisible Intelligence

Solomon, Grant, *The Scole Experiment*

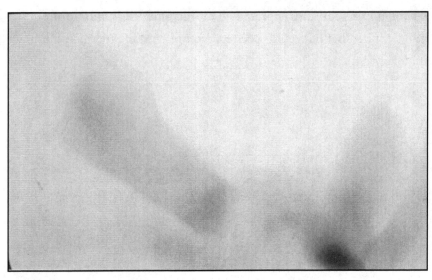

Spirit Flame Card (Medium Elaine Kuzmeskus)
Message: "A bridge broken in half—a broken relationship. Do not
worry as an angel is guiding you." The recipient of the spirit flame
card nodded, as she had recently met someone new after a bitter divorce.

Exercise: Spirit Flame Cards

One of my favorite ways to demonstrate physical mediumship is spirit flame
cards. I first saw them at Camp Lily Dale and later at Camp Chesterfield.
Spirit Flame messages are a form of physical phenomenon where spirit
guides produce an impression on a white card. After tuning into spirit, the
medium places a blank three-by-five-inch white index card over a candle
flame several times. Be careful to place the card close enough to form a picture but not so close as to catch on fire. Spirit will direct you to the recipient of the card.

Usually I receive messages for this person from the time I start the card
to the moment I put it in the sitter's hands. Use all your psychic skills—

intuition, clairaudience, and clairvoyance—as you do the spirit flame cards. Take a moment to use your mediumship to interpret the symbol for the sitter. Many of these cards are very evidential. For example, I did a workshop in the fall of 2009 at the Quincy Spiritualist Church in Quincy, Massachusetts, and three people received spirit flame card with trumpets to indicate their ability for trumpet mediumship.

Spirit Photography

If you wish to capture faces, orbs, or outlines of spirit on film, here are some suggestions. First it is important to gain rapport with spirit. Then you can take a picture with a conventional camera or a digital one. Be patient, as it sometimes takes many photographs to get an orb.

If you want to take the process a step farther, try solar plexus photography. Chesterfield medium Robert Channey, who worked in the 1940s, '50s, and '60s, used photographic paper, which he placed against his solar plexus in mediation. When he developed the film, an image would appear, often of a spirit guide or departed loved one.

Start by giving each person a three-by-five-inch piece of photographic paper. Ask the sitters to relax and enter a state of meditation in a dark room. Visualize the picture you desire. State clearly what picture you wish to receive. Continue to meditate for about ten minutes. When they are ready, each sitter should press the slick side of the paper against his or her solar plexus. Continue to meditate in silence for another ten minutes without distraction. Collect the exposed pieces of paper and place them in an envelope. Then have a photographer develop them or if possible develop them yourself.

Tom and Lisa Butler, directors of Association TransCommunication.

The Rev. Carl Hewitt, Spiritualist medium.

Spirit faces that manifested on portrait.

Photographer: Elaine Kuzmeskus

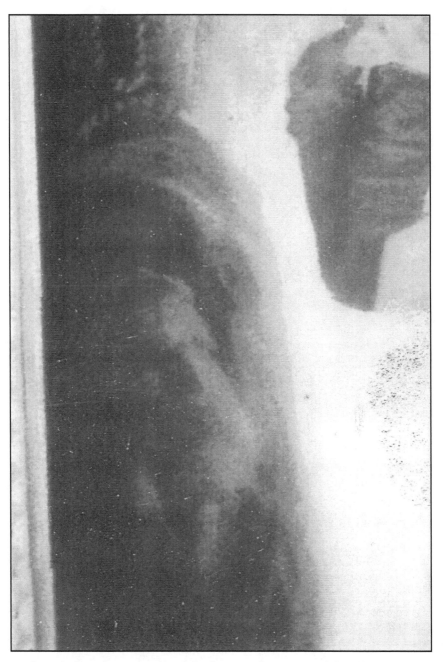

A bearded man appeared upside down in the corner of the photograph.

An angel manifests in flames as shaman Mary Arendt does a fire ceremony.

Orbs with faces.

Photographer: Paige Bushee

Orb photograph.

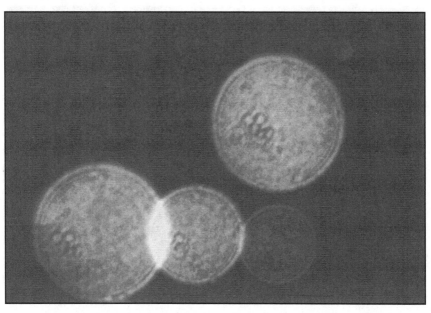

Close-up of orb photograph.

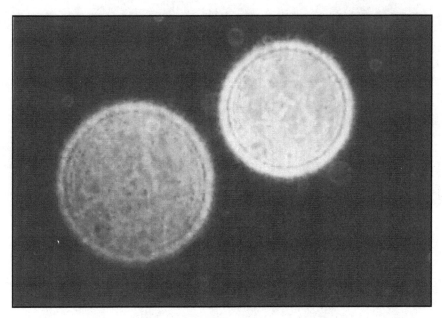

Details of orbs from Paige Bushee's photograph.

Psychic photo in front of house.

Photographer: Linda Willard

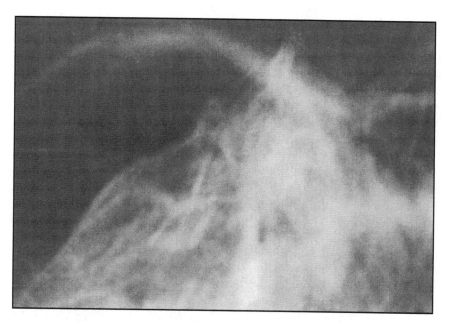

Linda Willard psychic photograph.

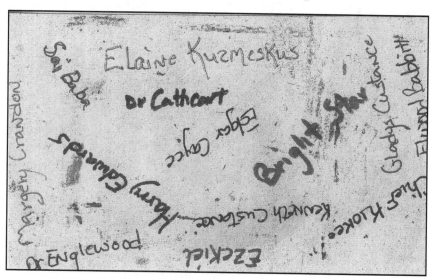

Names of author's guides that appeared on the back of spirit card.
Medium: the Rev. Hoyt Robinette.

A large Indian appeared in photo taken
at Cedar Hill Cemetery in Hartford, Connecticut.

Photographer: Donna Tomaslofski

The Rev. Hoyt Robinette, physical medium.

Ronald's precipitated spirit card with Mary and Joseph.
Medium: the Rev. Hoyt Robinette.

Author's precipitated spirit card with a portrait of Dr. Elmer Cathcart.
Medium: the Rev. Hoyt Robinette.

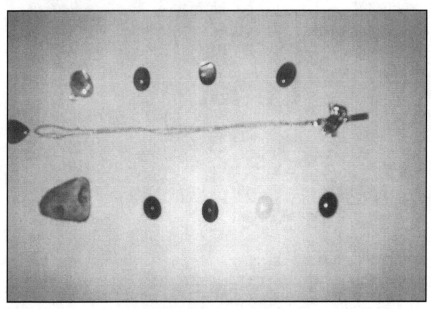

Gold cross apport received July 27, 2006, at a
trumpet séance conducted by the Rev. Hoyt Robinette.

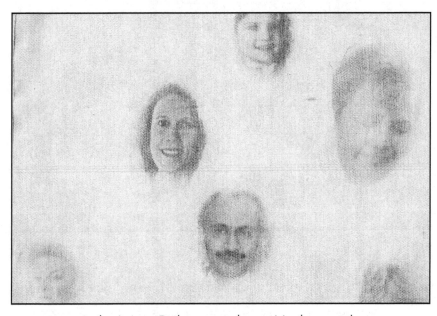

Author's Aunt Ruth appeared on spirit photograph.
Medium: the Rev. Hoyt Robinette.

Chapter Eleven

The Medium's Cabinet

Your belief will help create the fact.   —William James

I t wasn't long before I went from taking lessons in trance and table tipping to demonstrating for others. Often students would describe a bright golden light over my head as I began to channel. Sometimes the spirit of the Rev. Gladys Custance would be seen overshadowing and a higher-pitched voice would come through. At other times, a deep voice of a male would come out of my lips.

What does it feel like to go into trance? It feels like you are in a cocoon or almost like there are cobwebs over your face, and your mind still, your body in a paralyzed state of inertia. Then gradually, as trance deepens, I can feel spirit gain control of my vocal cords. Often there is a sensation of energy traveling down my body. On occasions, the face of a spirit would literally appear over my face. This is a process called transfiguration.

In order to facilitate transfiguration, I had my husband, Ron, construct what is known as a spirit cabinet. The concept of using a spirit cabinet dates back to the Davenport Brothers: Ira Erastus Davenport (1839–1911) and William Henry Davenport (1841–1877). They developed the idea of using a spirit cabinet, which became part of their stage act. The men would be tied up in the cabinet with ropes tied as tight as possible, to ensure that it was spirit hands that played the instruments placed in the cabinet.

Often the audience would hear musical instruments play and other phenomena. While some thought the act to be a magician's trick, Spiritualists believed the spirits were present to play musical instruments:

"Part of the brother's act was to look for volunteers from the audience who would then tie them up inside of the cabinet. Overeager skeptics often tied the Davenports with elaborate and painful knots that sometimes drew blood. In spite of this, once the cabinet doors were closed, wondrous spirit music filled the air from inside and disembodied hands would appear through apertures that had been left open on the exterior walls."[1]

Few mediums utilize a spirit cabinet on stage unless they are demonstrating transfiguration. One the premiere transfiguration mediums in recent years was England's Queenie Nixon (1918–1989). While in trance, Nixon was observed to have the physical features of the deceased transfigure over her face while she remained mute. When photographed with infrared photography, clouds of ectoplasm were captured on film.[2]

While I never had the privilege to witness Queenie Nixon's transfiguration, I was able to view the transfigurations of the Rev. Richard Schoeller. A tall, gracious man in his mid forties, the Reverend Schoeller was a funeral director on Long Island for eighteen years and now uses physical mediumship to give comfort to the bereaved and to obtain higher knowledge through spirit communication. Schoeller was initially surprised to discover he was a natural trance medium. When he took his pastoral training at Lily Dale Assembly, he and four other students decided to attend a trance class. The group arrived at the appointed time at the Assembly Hall and found five chairs arranged in a circle, but not a instructor. The fledgling mediums decided to try trance on their own. Before he knew it, Richard Scheoller was unconscious and channeling Azur, the spirit guide of the Campbell Brothers. He even assumed the hand position with two fingers of his right hand pointed up, as seen in the picture of Azur precipitated by the Campbell Brothers.

When I heard that the Rev. Richard Schoeller would be demonstrating trance and transfiguration mediumship March 28, 2009, at the local Spiritualist church, I was eager to see his work. After a lecture on transfiguration, Reverend Schoeller donned black pants and a black tee shirt and sat in a medium's cabinet. The group of forty watched in silence in the basement of the First Spiritualist Church of Springfield, Massachusetts, as the medium went into trance. The room was pitch dark with only a red light placed six feet from the Reverend Schoeller to illuminate the face of the medium.

As I focused on Schoeller's face, I saw spirit faces transfiguring over the medium's features. At first I saw a series of male faces. The first man looked like William James; then several other figures from the late 1800s followed.

Then two female faces—one looked like Emma Hardridge, a British trance medium from the late 1800s, and another also a brunette with a rounder build and hairstyle from the 1920s.

The faces transfigured rapidly—one about every ten seconds.

Many people in the audience excitedly identified faces of dead relatives. For instance, one gentleman called out, "That's my uncle! I know him from his face that had been scarred on one side."

While mediums such as the Reverend Schoeller use the cabinet for transfiguration, other mediums use a cabinet for materialization. One of the most famous of materialization mediums was Ethel Post-Parrish. On August 8, 1943, at Camp Silver Belle in Pennsylvania, she materialized several figures before an audience of twenty-five. The first to materialize was the medium's guide, Silver Belle, who promised, "I am going to work hard tonight and try to get as many of your loved ones through as possible." It wasn't long before the six-foot spirit of Silver Belle's grandfather, Chief Baconrind, emerged from the cabinet, accompanied by other spirits: "In rapid succession, the following phenomena occurred: Ella Carter and a Dr. Baker, both in spirit, materialized for Joseph Graham, Bryn Mawr, Pennsylvania. These two held the floor simultaneously and for several minutes talked to Mr. Graham. Ella

Carter moved from the center of the room to her right and stopped a few feet away from me. I could see that she was a very beautiful spirit."[3]

By the way, Ethel Post-Parrish's gatekeeper was her cousin, the Rev. Mable Ripple, who for many years was president of Camp Chesterfield. While materialization such as that of Ethel Post-Parrish is rare, working with a spirit cabinet is still in vogue at camp. When I visited Suzanne Greet in 2006 at the camp, she allowed me to sit in her cabinet. The energy was incredible. I immediately felt light-headed and ready for trance.

After my visit to Camp Chesterfield, I realized the importance of using a cabinet for physical phenomena. When we returned to Suffield, my husband and I began to look at pictures of old spirit cabinets in order to design one suitable for my office space. Ron cleverly put together a portable cabinet out of gray electrical pipe fittings, When the six-foot-high cabinet frame was completed, I had a black velvet curtain custom made to surround the frame and another piece fitted for the top.

By 2008 the cabinet was assembled. I placed it in the center of my office with a high-backed armchair from the dining room inside. Making the office dark enough for cabinet work turned out to be a challenge. First the students and I placed curtains made of blackout material on the windows and doorway. Next, a towel was wedged under the door so absolutely no light could shine in. In fact the only light allowed in the séance room was a red lamp.

Before we began our cabinet work, I went over the rules with the students. Rule number one: "Do not touch the medium while he or she is in trance. This could shock the medium and in extreme cases can cause injury."

To illustrate the point, I told the students about the late cabinet medium Helen Duncan, a Scottish housewife who traveled throughout wartime Britain giving séances in hundreds of Spiritualist churches and home circles. She became rather well known for her ability to materialize the spirits, who would appear in physical form, speak to, and touch their relatives: One poignant example of this occurred for Vincent Woodcock:

Vincent gave evidence in London's premier Old Bailey courtroom that the medium Helen Duncan slipped into trance and began producing the much scoffed at ectoplasm. Then his dead wife materialized from this ectoplasm matter and asked both Vincent and his sister-in-law to stand up. The materialized spirit then removed her wedding ring and placed it on her sister's wedding finger, adding, It is my wish that this takes place for the sake of my little girl. A year later the couple were married and returned for a further séance during which the dead woman appeared once more to give her renewed blessings to the happy couple.[4]

While many believed in Helen Duncan, the police did not. When they raided one materialization séance, Mrs. Duncan was abruptly seized while she was in a state of trance. The result was life-threatening burns on her body. Hence rule number one: Never touch a medium in trance.

The second rule has to do with preparation. Everyone in the cabinet circle is asked to meditate for an hour before the séance. Since many of our students have busy schedules, I suggest that they meditate within twenty-four hours of the cabinet séance, if they are unable to meditate that day.

Why is meditation so important? The guides tell us that they need to align our physical, mental, and spiritual bodies. The process is likened to stacking spools of thread. When in alignment, spirit can easily travel through the opening.

While the cabinet circle has not reached the level of materialization, a rare form of mediumship, we have done transfiguration in the cabinet with good results. The spirits of the Rev. Gladys Custance, the Rev. Arthur Ford, Margery Crandon, Dr. Mueller, Ivy (a British medium), and Gray Wolf (an American Indian), as well as Syl Seven, have manifested in the cabinet. Here are some of their comments:

Spirit Teacher advised the group on meditation during the September

10 Spirit Cabinet Seance:

> The teacher has to meditate within twenty-four hours of the class and would prefer as close to the class as possible. The medium meditates between three and four, but we realize that this is not possible for each person, and we don't wish to create anxiety surrounding meditation, so you choose the time within that time. And if you could meditate a bit each day as well that would be good, but we cannot adjust the body sufficiently unless we have a longer meditation and even if you do not go into dead trance, though many of you are, the fact that your body is inert, you have risen from the physical to at least the etheric or astral level and we can make the necessary adjustments.

> At the end of four cabinet séances, there are going to be some manifestations that you notice. There will be light flashes and a gray substance, not a solid substance, but a gray mist that will emanate from the cabinet and from the medium's solar plexus and what we are hoping to accomplish and a series of raps—Elwood Babbitt is in charge of this—the raps will come from the corner of the room. They are of such a nature that you will realize that they are a spirit rap. Have you not asked very definitely is this spirit and the rap will echo in reply. There will also be a greater gathering of light in the room. Look for the white light to come in very strong when the medium is with sprit. We ask that you keep a record of your internal experience in the trance. Keep a notebook and just afterwards, take five minutes and write the impressions that are internal because there are some who will make communication through the mental mediumship, and this would be very, very helpful. Expect the smell of violets. Expect the smell of roses to appear during the cabinet period.

On December 3, 2008, the spirit guides identified as Syl Seven gave this advice to the group:

> Elaine (in trance): We come in from the other side for each of you and to greet everyone that is here. We have with us the group known as Silbert Seven and this group is watching over us that group is progressive. We have to tell you the slowness and the deliberate pace is for the heart of the medium and for others that wish to develop this gift. Because her body can only take so much change—can only allow so much speeding up of vibration and hence we would be misusing the vehicles of those present if we were rush to open solar plexus connection. However, we are pleased that you are willing to meet in January and February because this will keep enough energy and juice flowing that we can continue with you throughout March, April, and May. We wish also to let you know that the e.t.s (extraterrestrials) have surrounded the room and that they indeed have helped to prepare before the Seven. We also have angelic presences and many in spirit who wish to assist. We are going to open for questions first.
>
> Student: What is the purpose of the group you belong to engaged in activity on the other side?
>
> Elaine: The group of seven and the extraterrestrials of Sirius are here to create a raising of the vibration, so greater intelligences can channel through not only healing but knowledge, which is important in the opening up of a pathway between your world and ours. It is a positive profound experience and it does take its toll on the material minded because it taxes their imagination that there is a finer energy that is operating and influencing the world of matter. Therefore knowledge of the spiritual world threatens the

very basis of this.

The spirit of Elwood Babbitt gave this advice:

> I have a great deal of difficulty controlling the apparatus of
> the medium's larynx, but I think there is sufficient control
> to speak. I am coming in because you have gone through a
> discouragement that I knew well in my own work. There
> is nothing that can be done other than moving forward and
> ignoring those who are of insufficient intelligence and are
> not ready for what we represent. There are so many seek-
> ing this higher knowledge of worlds beyond this one that
> are wishing to gain their freedom from the wheel of rebirth
> that it is not necessary to tarry because of them.
>
> We are working now physical phenomena that would
> help a period of time to arrange this [phenomenon], but
> this is the cause and effect. There are more opportunities
> for people in this group to develop clairaudience and the
> clairvoyance and there this time to be taken by any of these
> activities because it has been set aside not only by the medi-
> um but by her helpers.
>
> I am very busy because I am in charge of working as a
> guide for those who wish to develop channeling, so I am
> continuing the work I started. Charlie [Hapgood] has been
> working very hard with Daria [Babbitt] to get my books
> published to grow understanding of the books so there may
> be a greater fairness of humanity. We are also concerned
> about our coming earth changes about flooding especial-
> ly in the Carolinas, Mississippi, the Baja peninsula in
> California. We are concerned about violence in the cities.
> We are concerned in the coming months of a complete col-
> lapse of the health care system in major cities. Hence these
> things are on the horizon and require a consideration of

those who wish to serve.

Student: Are there going to be earth changes on the East Coast in December?

Elwood: We feel there could be more discouragement in the February [2009] month due to the stock market and Iraq, lack of resources, and unemployment in the cities. The greater issue is what happens in the Middle East in July, which has to be watched very carefully.

Later that evening a spirit identified as Mamie came in:

Mamie: I come in because I am very glad to see this group and I am amazed that more people are not interested because in my day many people came to Camp Chesterfield specifically to train for the mental and physical mediumship. It seems like things have changed so much—so much skepticism. that it has been put aside, but we are happy you are interested and we are here.

I know it takes a while, but sometimes when the physical starts to manifest it is very strong. And that is when the ectoplasm is at its height And it is beginning to connect in the cabinet. The cabinet must be completely dark; even a speck of light reduces the manifesting.

The spirit cabinet not only can be used for trance mediumship but for materialization as well. Mediums such as the late Helen Duncan and today's Stewart Alexander are famous for their materialization. While today's Spiritualist camps, for the most part do not have spirit cabinets, in their heyday there were quite a few. For instance, Camp Cassadaga attracted stellar mediums in the 1920s such as the famous physical medium, Mabel Riffle. Her Sunday-evening séances brought the largest audiences ever recorded at Cassadaga. No wonder. Typically for forty minutes at a time, the great message bearer would roll out name after name, fact after fact, in an endless stream that delighted the audience, confounded the critics, and filled investigators with wonder.[5] As Cassadaga grew in popularity, even the wife of Florida Senator Duncan Fletched defended Spiritualism before a House subcommittee, and later in 1926 published a book on the subject: *Death Unveiled.*[6]

With such a rich history, Ron and I were excited at the prospect of attending the Saturday night orb tour. The highlight was a visit to Colby Temple, which houses a séance room that the old-time mediums used for physical phenomena.

While only physical mediums were allowed in the room, tourists were allowed to take photographs from the doorway. Shivers went up my spine as we peered in. Apparently Ron and I were not alone, as seen in a series of photographs showing an eight-foot column of white ectoplasm in the center of the séance room. The column was literally moving across the room

End Notes

1. http://www.prairieghosts.com/davenport.html
2. Occultism & Parapsychology Encyclopedia. *Encyclopedia of Occultism and Parapsychology*
3. Jay Strong, "Ethel Post-Parrish Carried From The Cabinet While In Trance"
4. http://www.helenduncan.org.uk/helenstory/helenstory.html
5. John Gunthrie Jr., Phillip Charles De Lucas, Gary Monroe, *Cassadaga: the South's Oldest Spiritualist Camp*, University of Florida Press, Gainesville, FL, 2000, page 47
6. John Gunthrie Jr., Phillip Charles De Lucas, Gary Monroe,*Cassadaga: the South's Oldest Spiritualist Camp*, University of Florida Press, Gainesville, FL, 2000, page 48

Suggested Reading

Geley, Gustave, *Clairvoyance and Materialisation*
Harrison, Tom, *Life After Death: Living Proof*
Heathcote-James, Emma, *They Walk Among Us*
Sargent, Epes, *Proof Palpable of Immortality*
Vandersande, Jan W., *Life After Death*
Baron von Schrenck Notzing, *Phenomena of Materialization*

Instructions for a Spirit Cabinet

Materials:

    Gray electrical pipe and fittings

    8 3/4" tees

    8 3/4"-long turn ells

    8 3/4" x 10-foot gray electrical pipe

    Small can of plastic cement

Reminder: Do not cement four posts, so you can take it apart.

Height: 6 feet 2 inches

Length: 5 feet

Width: 4 feet

Start by assembling the pipes to make a base five by four feet. Then make a top five by four feet out of pipes, and connect the base to the top with six-foot two-inch pipes To do this use four cups, each placed in a corner. Once the base is assembled, drape black curtains and place a black curtain over the top. Finally, place a chair with arms in the cabinet, so the medium can relax completely and meditate.

    If you wish to contact spirit, meditate on a regular basis preferably at the same time and place. Have the medium sit in the cabinet with the curtains drawn. Assign two advanced students on either side of the cabinet to act as attendants. Turn off all lights. Begin with a prayer, then start singing some lively songs such as "Jingle Bells" or "I've Been Working on the Railroad" to lift the vibrations. Once spirit has entered the medium, the spirit will often allow a red lamp to be turned on, so when spirit is ready open the curtains and turn on the red light. If no permission is given the séance can be conducted in total darkness. However red light is needed to observe transfiguration. In either event, be sure to turn on the tape recorder for the medium's trance messages.

Spirit cabinet with trumpet on table.

Author visited Spiritualist Camp Cassadaga in January 2010.

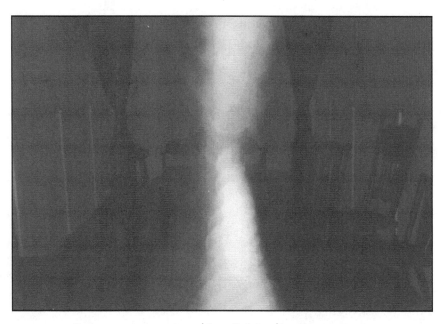

Energy vortex appeared in a Spiritualist séance room.

Photograph by Ronald Kuzmeskus

Ethel Post-Parrish in trance, materializing her guide Silver Belle.

Chapter Twelve

Healing Grief

People are like stained-glass windows. They sparkle and shine when the sun is out, but when the darkness sets in their true beauty is revealed only if there is light from within.

—Dr. Elisabeth Kübler-Ross

During my thirty-five years as a medium, I encountered profound grief and psychological depression. Fortunately, early in my career, I decided to use a five-thousand-dollar settlement I had received for my car accident in 1971 to return to college to and pursue a degree in counseling. I was more than a little nervous when I entered the University of Hartford in 1975. To be honest, I thought that I would be thrown out of the program if anyone found out that I was a medium.

In a way, it regrettable more counselors are not open to mediums. On his deathbed, Dr. Sigmund Freud said that, if he had his life to live over, he would study parapsychology. According to Freud, death is the prototype for all anxiety. Our fear of death is the deepest fear we face. *How sad,* I thought. *It is really just a transition to another world.*

I don't think my professors would have approved of mediumship. In fact, I knew they didn't. When we were asked to write our greatest fear on a card and place it in the box, I wrote, "I am the most afraid that people will find out that I am a medium." The professor, who by the way was my advisor, knew I was the one who had written the card. He accused me of taking counseling training as foil for mediumship. Nothing could be further from the truth. I believe both are valid. It is comforting to know that we exist past the change called death; however, some still need psychological help in times of grief and confusion.

Not only did I remain in the program but I was graduated in May of 1978 with a Masters in Counseling from the University of Hartford in Connecticut. Since then I have obtained a license as an LPC, Licensed Professional Counselor. Occasionally, I find my clairvoyance to be helpful with psychiatric patients. For example, I don't have to ask if a patient is experiencing auditory or visual hallucination; I can see by the presence or absence of light over their head. If the lights are present someone beyond the earth plane is contacting the patient either through voices or other hallucination. Also, I find my unshakable belief in a life after death helps to deal with those who are suicidal. Suicide may end life on earth, but it sends the perpetrator into a great state of confusion on the other side. According to spirit, often a person who commits suicide (which is a crime against the soul) is put on hold until their natural lifetime is completed.

More often, it is as a medium that I find blending the fields most useful. While demonstrating that loved ones continue to exist past the change called death is healing in itself, the bereaved need psychological guidance as well. Dr. Elisabeth Kübler-Ross delineates five stages of death and dying which can apply to grieving as well: denial, anger, bargaining, depression, and acceptance.

She was also open to mediumship. In her autobiography, *Wheel of Life*, Dr. Kübler-Ross shared her experience of assisting the terminally ill. Things were not always easy for the young doctor with the heavy European accent. Many of her fellow physicians misunderstood her desire to work with dying patients and viewed her work as a morbid fascination. In fact, she was about to abandon her project, when she had an unusual encounter in the halls of her Chicago hospital. Who should appear but Mary, a patient who had died ten months earlier! They walked back to Dr. Kübler-Ross's office. Mary took a seat and began to thank her doctor and the Rev. Rennie Gaines, a Unitarian minister who had assisted Dr. Kübler-Ross, for their assistance with Swartz's dying. Mary urged her "not to give up your work on death and dying—not yet." Mrs. Swartz continued, "Your work has just begun. We will help you." In *Wheel of Life*, Dr. Kübler-Ross described her reaction to the spirit of her deceased patient:

> All of a sudden, I sensed she knew my thoughts and every-thing I was going to say. I decided to ask her for proof that she was really there by giving her a pen and a sheet of paper and asked her to compose a brief note to Rev. Gaines. She scribbled a quick thank you. "Are you satisfied?" she asked.[1]

Later Dr. Kübler-Ross compared the signature on the note with the signature on Mary Schwartz's hospital record. When the two signatures matched, she became a firm believer in life after death. In fact, Dr. Kübler-Ross advised her patients to learn to get in touch with the silence within themselves and know that everything in this life has a purpose. There are no mistakes, no coincidences; all events are blessings given to us to learn from.

Dr. Kübler-Ross pioneered the field of thanatology, which is a gift to the many who suffer from prolonged or painful illnesses. These patients can work through the stages of death and dying with the help of trained coun-selors. When death occurs, those who return report release. How often I hear the voice of a spirit say, "I knew I was dead because I was no longer in pain," or " I knew I had passed over, as I was able to breathe freely." When a loved one is suffering, please pray for a peaceful passing.

This was my prayer for my eighty-nine-year-old mother, Dorothy Courtney, during the last year of her life. When she did pass over in her sleep at the age of eighty-nine, I felt God had answered my prayers. Still, her memorial service was a very emotional event for me. In fact, when the Reverend Robin asked if I wished to say a few words, I demurred: "I couldn't possibly." However, something stirred in me when the minister asked if anyone in the congregation would like to share a memory. I stood up and shared a few vignettes. It was the last thing I could do for my mother in this life. Besides, the spirit of my stepfather, John Courtney, who had died in 1992, pushed me forward.

Grief is difficult, even for a medium. I remember, asking my mother to step back as I would start to cry every time I thought about her. This did not sit well with my deceased mother. A few days after her death, March 6, 2008, my four year-old granddaughter, Meredith, went into the bathroom and called out: "Mom, there's lady in here." Her mother, Heather, not keen on spirits, sent her four-year-old son, Will, in to investigate.

"Yeah, Mom," Will called out, "there's an old lady here." When Heather questioned him, he described my mother, whom he had not seen in great detail.

I laughed when my daughter told me the story. "Why didn't you go into the bathroom yourself to investigate?" My lawyer daughter just shrugged. "You know I don't believe in that kind of stuff." Touched by the great effort my mother had made to materialize before my grandchildren, I sent the thought out immediately, "Momma, you can come through any time you wish."

The story illustrates an important point: spirit makes a great effort to come through out of love for those left behind. However, it is also necessary to be receptive to the spirit's vibration. As a medium, I was receptive, but too overwhelmed with grief to communicate.

People often ask me how long they should wait before making contact. Spirits can communicate immediately. In fact, they are eager to reach out to those they love. Often they come through in the first critical hours after death. I frequently see the spirit of the deceased standing right next to their relatives as mourners pass by the coffin.

Sometimes there needs to be an acceptance of the passing before communication can come through, either in dreams or intuitive experiences. Also, spirit takes time to adjust to death. If you visit a medium too soon, the spirit of your loved one may not have sufficient energy to manifest, yet our spirit people do wish to communicate through a medium. Most often they are determined to let you know that they are still part of your life. Messages describe everyday events that occurred after their passing, such as picking out a dress or the birth of a baby. Details are described by spirit just to let you know that they were present on the other side.

Here are some suggestions for healing grief:

1. Take time to grieve in your own way. It is not unusual for a widow or widower to need a year to assimilate the loss of a spouse.

2. Accept that your loss is real. While your loved one is not dead, he or she is no longer available to you. It is okay to cry or feel pain.

3. Learn to adjust to life without the deceased. While death does not end a relationship, it does require adjustment. It is natural to miss shared activities.

4. Be willing to seek support.

5. Learn to cherish memories. Perhaps you can put an album or collection together, or even a scholarship in your loved one's name.

6. Allow yourself to move on. For some this may mean a physical move, for others allowing new people into their lives. As you begin to enjoy new experiences, you can take comfort in your cherished memories. Take comfort in the love you shared, but remember living well is a compliment to your loved one.

For most people, the hardest part of grieving is learning what to do with all the love they shared. When you lose a parent, a spouse, a friend, or a pet, remind yourself that love does not end at the grave. Love is eternal. When a memory comes to mind, send a loving thought out and know it is received on the other side.

When it comes to death, perhaps the poet should have the last word. Kahlil Gibran captured its essence most eloquently in his book *The Prophet:*

> For what is it to die, but to stand naked in the wind and
>   melt into the Sun?
> And what is it to cease breathing but to free the breath from
>   its restless
> Tides so it may rise and seek God unencumbered?

End Notes

1. Dr. Elisabeth Kübler-Ross, *Wheel of Life*, Touchstone Books, New York, NY, page 177.

Suggested Reading

George Anderson, *We Don't Die*

Damion Brinkley, *Saved By the Light*

Hugh Lynn Cayce and Edgar Cayce, *Death: God's Other Door*

Betty Eadie, *Embraced By the Light*

Geoffrey Hodson, *Through the Gateway of Death*

Dr. Elisabeth Kübler-*Ross Wheel of Life*

Stephen Levine, *Who Dies?*

Dr. Raymond Moody, *Life After Life*

Reunions

Howard Murphet, *Death: The Undiscovered Country*

Jenny Randles and Peter Hough, *Life After Death and the World Beyond*

Dr. Kenneth Ring, *The Omega Experience*

Tom Shroder, *Old Souls*

Dr. Ian Stevenson, *Twenty Cases Suggestive of Reincarnation*

James Van Praagh,*Healing Grief: Reclaiming Life After Any Loss*

John White, *A Practical Guide to Death and Dying*

Obituary Exercise

Since we are such a death-denying society, another exercise that I use in Psychology of Death and Dying is the Obituary Exercise. Set aside about an hour of time and mentally imagine your death. Where are you? How old do you feel you are? Then with the full knowledge that death is but a transition to higher life, take a moment and think of how you would like the world to remember you. What were your greatest accomplishments? Now, take these notes and write your own obituary. While this is not an easy exercise, it is an important one to help you get in touch with your feelings about death and dying.

Electronic Voice Phenomena (EVP) Exercise

Frederick Jurgenson demonstrated that it is possible to captured spirit voices on tape. If you also wish to try to capture spirit on tape, you will need a tape recorder, tapes, and a doctor's stethoscope. Choose a quiet time each day to practice. Sit in silent meditation with the tape playing. Send the thought out to spirit you wish to communicate. Since the voices come in faintly at first, use the doctor's stethoscope to check for sounds.

Dr. Elisabeth Kübler-Ross.

Ronald's precipitated spirit card with picture of a city on the other side.
Medium: The Rev. Hoyt Robinette.

Index

To order additional copies of this book,
please send full amount plus $5.00 for
postage and handling for the first book and
$1.00 for each additional book.
Minnesota residents add 7.125 percent sales tax

Send orders to:

Galde Press
PO Box 460
Lakeville, Minnesota 55044-0460

Credit card orders call 1–800–777–3454
Fax (952) 891–6091
Visit our website at *www.galdepress.com*
and download our free catalog,
or write for our catalog.